CAREERS in

EDUCATION

VGM Professional Careers Series

EDUCATION

ALAN J. REIMAN, ED.D., and ROY A. EDELFELT, ED.D.

FOURTH EDITION

VGM Career Books

*Chicago New York San Francisco Lisbon London Madrid Mexico City
Milan New Delhi San Juan Seoul Singapore Sydney Toronto*

Library of Congress Cataloging-in-Publication Data

Reiman, Alan.
    Careers in education / Alan Reiman and Roy Edelfelt—4th ed.
       p.   cm.—(VGM professional careers series)
    Includes bibliographical references.
    ISBN 0-07-140578-X
    1. Education—Vocational guidance—United States. 2. Teaching—
Vocational guidance—United States. I. Reiman, Alan. II. Title.
III. Series.

LB1775.2.E37   2004
370'.23'73—dc21   2003050177

1 2 3 4 5 6 7 8 9 0 DOC/DOC 2 1 0 9 8 7 6 5 4 3

ISBN 0-07-140578-X

Interior design by Robert S. Tinnon

McGraw-Hill books are available at special quantity discounts to use as premiums and sales promotions, or for use in corporate training programs. For more information, please write to the Director of Special Sales, Professional Publishing, McGraw-Hill, Two Penn Plaza, New York, NY 10121-2298. Or contact your local bookstore.

This book is printed on acid-free paper.

CONTENTS

ACKNOWLEDGMENTS

Collecting the information to revise this book required the help of many people and organizations. Not only did the task entail covering eight types of education careers, it also involved gathering details on subcategories of those careers.

For the first time, we had substantial assistance from the websites of organizations, agencies, and associations. Websites were easy to access, well developed, and loaded with information. In many cases we missed contact with live people. That was a new experience, both efficient and convenient but also dehumanizing. Talking with representatives of organizations always has yielded unexpected information, unusual ideas, and the enthusiasm and the commitment that people convey about their specialty.

Nevertheless, we had numerous conversations with real people in many of the jobs we explored. So we did not miss out entirely on the richness of personal contact, and we appreciate the research assistance of Valerie Smith.

We are deeply indebted to all the people and organizations that contributed information and ideas. We hope that the book promotes information and interest for those considering a career in education.

This edition contains a new feature in each chapter: a firsthand account from a person who has "been there, done that" in the career being described. We list all the contributors below and express our gratitude to them for sharing their perceptions.

- Chan Evans, special educator, Augusta State University (GA)
- Jean Fleming, adult educator, College of the Southwest (Hobbs, NM)
- Ron Gager, management consultant, Boulder, CO
- Lisa Johnson, public school teacher, Wake County Public Schools (NC)
- Paul Keene, central office administrator, Durham County Public Schools (NC)
- Deborah Neely, public school teacher, Cincinnati Public Schools (OH)
- Jim Palermo, principal, Wake County Public Schools (NC)
- Allen Schmieder, federal agency staff member, U.S. Department of Education, Washington, DC
- Amy Shapiro, college professor, Alverno College (WI)
- Allen Warner, university professor, University of Houston

The authors also acknowledge the significant contributions of Margo Johnson, who edited the manuscript. Her patience and editorial acumen have been invaluable.

AN INTRODUCTION TO CAREERS IN EDUCATION

In the United States, education is the underpinning of the culture, the basis of the quality of life. Now, more than ever, it is one of the country's top priorities: in 2002, Congress passed and President George W. Bush signed the No Child Left Behind Act, legislation intended to improve the education of American children. Universal and free public education to age eighteen is a foundation of American democracy. An informed, literate, and compassionate citizenry is essential to maintaining and improving the condition of the American people and to assisting other nations in raising their standards of living. Those convictions have long been commitments of educators, but now the public and businesspeople, as well as political leaders, concur.

In a country of more than 280 million people, public education alone is an immense undertaking, and public and private education together are a gigantic enterprise. The total expenditure for public and private education in schools, colleges, and universities is more than $700 billion per year. In the 1999–2000 school year, total expenditures made by public school districts came to nearly $382 billion. Expenditures on training and development in business and industry exceeded $54 billion. The outlay for adult and continuing education is difficult to define but must be large, given that 55 million people enrolled in adult education courses in 1999.

Formal education institutions (public and private) employ more than 4.6 million people in teaching roles in elementary, secondary, and higher education. They employ another 6 million in administrative, professional, and support staff roles. The number of instructors and teachers involved in adult and continuing education in business, industry, government, and other entities is, again, difficult to define, but also must be enormous. In these fields, part-time and short-term employment of people is a common practice. An estimate for business and industry alone is 75,000.

Most educators still are teachers, but many specialty areas have developed. Some involve teaching, but others do not. Reading teachers, school counselors, librarians and media specialists, nurses, physical therapists, social workers, business managers, instructional technology educators, deans of student affairs, and public relations officers are just a few of the many education professionals.

Of course, there also are administrators for all levels and units of education, from preschool to higher education, building to district, department to institution, university to system, and local plant to corporate headquarters.

Developments in society have created a number of new areas in which education is needed. Some of these developments represent progress; others present challenges; still others reflect problems. All of them generate new opportunities for learning and for attacking ignorance. They create new careers in education as schools, colleges, and other agencies offer types of instruction that provide enlightenment. Developments that represent progress include innovation, information technologies, robotics, and instructional technologies, including technologies applied in education. Developments that present challenges include coping with threats of terrorism, the demand for principled integrity and responsibility in the professional workplace, the special needs of people of color and non-English-speaking youngsters and adults, the increasing population of elderly people, and the continued presence of parochialism in a world that is ever more complex and interconnected. Developments that represent the problems that education must address are the spread of AIDS, drug and alcohol abuse, differences in the quality of education in rich and poor schools, teenage unemployment, environmental degradation, and poverty. New and continued attention is being given to education for parenthood, intervention at preschool ages, career changes, dropout prevention and reentry, and prisoner rehabilitation.

Changes in some fields are swift. Teachers of instructional technology became necessary in less than a decade, but educators have yet to agree on just what computer literacy and technology involve and on what can and should be taught in schools. Only now are states identifying curriculum goals in technology literacy.

Adult and continuing education, whether undertaken for personal fulfillment or organizational profit, reflects the persistent need for people to acquire new knowledge and skills to remain effective in a changing society. The boundaries of education have expanded far beyond the school and the college or university. Indeed, distance education knows few boundaries. Education is part of almost every institution, agency, and organization in American society: business, industry, government, the military, professional associations, and all types of cultural and service agencies. In fact, the pace of societal and technological change has made continuing education essential for almost all citizens.

All education requires people to deliver it, including teachers, administrators, managers, and counselors. More people now are engaged in education of one sort or another than in any other occupation in American society.

Education, then, is a *dominant career* in the United States. It also is rising in importance and status. Long a second-fiddle profession that did not offer adequate prestige or good pay, education finally is coming to the fore. Increasingly, citizens and policy makers realize that high-quality education is related to a vibrant democracy, quality of life, innovation, and global competitiveness. Although some people continue to express concern that American schools limit the nation's competitive position in the world market, a recent report of the World Economic Forum indicates that the United States ranks second in the world on the forum's Current Competitiveness Index, trailing only Finland. Further, the United States' top scores are on a set of variables that make up what the forum calls *national innovation capacity*. U.S. and Canadian elementary, secondary, and postsecondary schools have developed a culture that encourages innovative thinking.

Institutions and agencies offering education include the following:

- Preschools
- Public and private K–12 schools
- Vocational-technical schools
- Two- and four-year colleges and universities
- Graduate and professional schools
- Institutes
- Business and industry

- Federal government colleges, academies, and universities
- Military schools
- Adult and continuing education programs
- Arts and crafts schools

This book gives attention to almost all of these, except schools for strictly vocational-technical or military training, and schools largely devoted to preparing artists, musicians, and craftspeople (for example, the Rhode Island School of Design, the Juilliard School, and the Cranbrook Academy of Art).

Teaching is the central career in education; all other educators exist to support teachers in one way or another. Teaching also is one of the most difficult human endeavors. Most memorable teachers share one trait: they are truly present in the classroom, deeply engaged with their students and their subject.

Because teaching is the usual entry point to other careers in education, this book gives special attention to teaching at different levels and in various types of educational institutions. Further, it emphasizes public school teaching in kindergarten through grade 12 because that is by far the largest educational enterprise.

Jobs that entail teaching vary so widely that generalizing about them as a single phenomenon is not reasonable. Some characteristics, however, apply to teaching anywhere and in any mode:

1. It involves a teacher and a learner.
2. Good teaching comes from the intellect, the identity, and the integrity of the teacher.
3. The teacher has a special expertise. Part of it is in-depth knowledge of subject matter; part is a knowledge of teaching itself; and part is a knowledge of the learner.
4. Teachers (even those in profit-making institutions) are committed to enlightenment. They want their students to learn.
5. Teachers have a responsibility to contribute to the welfare of society.
6. Teachers have ethics and standards of scholarship, which include considering the available data, treating data and issues objectively, reporting findings fairly, and respecting the privacy of students.

Because teaching is the entry point for any career in education, a brief historical perspective on teaching in America is appropriate.

The Colonial Period

Most teachers in the colonial period taught until something better came along. Teaching was generally viewed as a temporary position, and teachers were deemed acceptable (or unacceptable) on the basis of their religious preference and their moral and civic commitments. Before the American Revolution, teachers were required to sign oaths of allegiance to the crown of England. When the Revolution started, the oath of allegiance was changed to the state in which the teacher resided.

Although teachers were expected to maintain high moral standards, the public typically had very low expectations for teachers' professional preparation. There were no specialized schools, and a teacher was expected to know only slightly more than students. Thus began the joke of the teacher being only one page ahead of the students.

The status and the salaries of teachers were proportional to the age of their students. Therefore, college teachers were granted the highest status and largest salaries, secondary school teachers lower status and smaller salaries, and elementary school teachers the lowest status and lowest salaries. Typically, schools were poorly equipped, and students attended irregularly. Thus the school term was short, making teaching a part-time vocation. The turnover rate for teachers was exceedingly high, and that contributed to keeping the status of teachers low.

The Nineteenth Century

One of the exciting developments of the early nineteenth century was common schools, now known as public schools. The Revolution brought with it a new vision of universal education—that is, schooling for everyone. The country's founders realized that a democratic government was only as strong as the people's capacity to make informed decisions, and that in turn raised the need for basic education. (Universal education at this time was meant only for whites. However, the same arguments were used later to extend basic education to racial and ethnic minorities and children who are disabled or gifted.)

Teacher salaries continued to be very low, and the status of teaching remained largely unchanged from colonial times. However, a slow change occurred in the professionalism of teaching. The first teacher education institutions, called *normal schools*, were created in 1823. *Normal* referred to instructing teachers in the norms, or methods, of teaching. Normal schools provided specialized training in teaching methods and grew in number. Following the Civil War, a greater demand for public secondary education led to the continued growth of normal schools.

The Twentieth Century

The first sixty years of the twentieth century witnessed a number of important changes. Normal schools grew into teachers colleges, which quadrupled in number from 1920 to 1940. However, some two- and three-year training programs for teachers survived until the early 1970s.

Progressive education was created and studied in the early 1900s. Championed by John Dewey, it was a formalized attempt to reform education radically through implementation of principles that now seem commonplace: a focus on the natural interest of the student as the best motive for school work; the teacher as a guide or a facilitator rather than a dispenser of information; a broad curriculum to foster both learning and development; the school being responsible for tending to students' general health and physical development; and school and home working together to meet students' needs.

These curricular methods were carefully tested in the Eight-Year Study, carried out in the 1930s. This important and careful comparison study found that high schools that employed activity- and problem-based curriculum using instructional approaches such as small groups, cooperative learning, inquiry, simulations, and field trips yielded students with higher grades, more academic honors, more student engagement and intellectual curiosity, greater responsibility, and increased participation in student groups than high schools that did not employ this type of curriculum. Unfortunately, the results were published in 1942, during World War II, and the exciting findings were obscured as the nation became preoccupied with war and postwar recovery. As a result, the high school as an institution continued with little change.

The 1950s also witnessed a return to greater emphasis on subject matter, which began in earnest after the Russian satellite *Sputnik* was launched. Reform in education is cyclical and often is influenced more by political whim than by scientific policy.

Another significant change, occurring during the 1950s and 1960s, was the direction of major attention to students with special needs. For example, curriculum reform movements focused on "culturally disadvantaged" children, and the federal government provided significant additional financial support to change schools so that they could better address the needs of these children. Head Start and Title I programs are examples of such federally funded efforts.

Junior high schools, or middle schools, saw major growth in the twentieth century. Indeed, since the middle 1980s, there has been a deepening commitment to the improvement of education for early adolescents, with a strong emphasis on the intellectual, social-emotional, and moral and character development of students.

Still another major change occurred in teacher education. Teacher training came to be called *teacher education*, and by the early 1970s a four-year-college degree was the standard. Public concern about teacher competency and the professional status of teachers will most likely prompt expectations for even more education and higher standards of teacher competence. Indeed, many educators now want to add a fifth year to teacher preparation. However, the recent dramatic shortages of teachers could undermine such aspirations as states struggle to find enough teachers for today's schools.

WHY CHOOSE A CAREER IN EDUCATION?

In the best circumstances, a career in education is challenging, inspiring, and rewarding. Whether or not it becomes so depends on what a person expects or wants from such a career and how deliberately he or she sets out to find employment that will satisfy those desires. This book is designed to help people explore professions in education by providing information, opinions, and other sources of data that will promote a deliberate process of weighing and choosing.

Teaching

Many people choose teaching (and remain teachers) because they care deeply about their subject, be it English, chemistry, engineering, or another area. Teaching is one way to pursue an intellectual attraction to a field. A person learns any subject better and in greater depth by teaching it. College professors, in particular, are committed to study and research in their discipline. However, action research now is being conducted in K–12 classrooms as well. The job of any teacher, any educator, requires study throughout a career.

Another reason that people are drawn to teaching is that they like working with young people. They find nurturing the growth and development of the young to be one of life's greatest challenges. Every class comes down to this connection between teacher and students, face to face, engaged in the most ancient of professions. Caring for students excites good teachers, challenges most, and requires all to examine and understand a diversity of student experiences, ethnic traditions, learning styles, and developmental needs. Teachers tend to be altruistic about contributing to the development of the next generation.

Teaching will likely prove to be a satisfying career for anyone who is keen on a subject, committed to helping students learn and develop, and intrigued with the thinking and learning processes. The teaching and learning processes also change as teachers continue to learn and understand who they are. Self-understanding and integrity are critical to good teaching.

Many careers in education begin with teaching in an elementary or secondary school, or a college or university. This is true of virtually all public school administrators, from assistant principal to superintendent, and of specialists and supervisors whose entry-level function involves instruction (as opposed to, say, diagnosis and treatment). It also is true of many private school administrators, specialists, and supervisors, and of many administrators in higher education and educators in government and business.

On the practical side, people often choose teaching because it has job security once they have earned tenure (and for public school teachers, a regular teaching credential). Some are attracted by what appears to be an easy work schedule—for example, for teachers in elementary and secondary schools, a five-and-a-half-hour workday with students, a work year of forty weeks, and time off at Christmas or Hanukkah, in the spring, and on all legal holidays. Appearances are deceiving, however. Public school teachers work incredibly hard. Most teachers work more than fifty hours a week. Further, working conditions rarely are optimal. Too little time is set aside for planning instruction, and many demands compete for a teacher's time. Public school teachers get little time for lunch at any level of school. Elementary school teachers typically teach the same children for the entire day and have little time for lunch. In many cases they supervise students during lunch. Secondary school teachers have short lunch periods as well, but they rarely supervise students during lunch.

The exodus of beginning teachers from schools is another clue that working conditions are not ideal. Data from the National Center for Education Statistics' 2002 Schools and Staffing Survey of more than 50,000 teachers nationwide indicate that 29 percent of teachers leave after three years on the job, and 39 percent after five years. After five years the rate of exodus levels off. The average annual turnover rate for teachers is 13.2 percent, whereas the average attrition rate in other professions is 11 percent. Interestingly, public school teachers leave the field at a rate of 12.4 percent a year, while the annual exit rate of private school teachers is 18.9 percent, and of those in small private schools, 22.8 percent. When teachers were asked why they departed, the largest groups—40 percent from urban schools and 49 percent from private schools—said that they did so for personal reasons, such as deciding to stay home to raise children.

The notion that summers are free is a myth for many teachers. The off-season often is occupied with advanced study, fulfillment of local or state inservice education requirements, or travel to enlarge perspective.

Teachers in higher education are drawn to the profession for many of the reasons stated for K–12 teachers, and for others as well. They value the intellectual freedom and interaction, the opportunity continually to seek greater depth of knowledge in their field, the relative autonomy in their workplace, and the chance to do research. The work schedule, though rigorous, is very appealing. Although faculty must be present for classes, maintain a certain number of office hours with students, and participate in various meetings, they can come and go as they please, doing their preparations, research, reading, and related activities wherever they wish.

Special Services

Because of the great diversity of specialists and their wide deployment, it is difficult to generalize about why people do or should choose careers as specialists. Specialists are personnel in public schools and colleges who are not regular classroom teachers but who have expertise in an area critical to schooling, such as reading, speech-language pathology and audiology, special education, and psychology. They may teach, but they also consult with teachers and parents and engage in a number of other activities.

School specialists have latitude beyond that of most school personnel, particularly if they are itinerant teachers, and that is one reason the career is appealing. Specialists in higher education may have less freedom of activity than their academic colleagues. A psychologist serving as a counselor to college students, for example, may have full-day office hours on most or all days.

Music, art, and physical education specialists are similar to other school specialists in regard to latitude and thus offer a good example. They can have unique work schedules. Most regular classroom teachers (and even administrators) are tied to a building. Classes come one after another, at the same time of day, day in and day out, for forty weeks per year. But many music and art teachers travel from one building to another and thus have a different schedule almost every day. They get out into the air between assignments. They interact with a wide variety of teachers. They eat in a variety of lunchrooms. They teach children in different grades, K–4, K–6, even K–12.

Physical education teachers can work outdoors, weather permitting. Music teachers can teach classes and work with performance groups as well. Art teachers can work with accomplished high school students in a studio situation and still teach beginners in general art in the elementary school.

Administration or Supervision

Most people become educators because they want to help young people grow and develop and because they want to participate in academic life. They are committed to the intellectual process, to the importance of thinking and reasoning, to the discovery and advancement of knowledge. Educators think first about what they can do to meet those commitments.

Administrators or supervisors attempt to facilitate groups of teachers in reaching such goals. The attraction is the possibility of exercising leadership that motivates others to improve their performance in helping students learn. The word *facilitate* is key. Administrators who see themselves as riding a white horse and leading a charge are usually reined in by those they lead, who often are as able and insightful as they are. Further, and particularly in higher education, the protocols of academic life ensure freedom to challenge and contest, the right to voice diverse theories and rationales, and protection for those who take issue with or resist administrative decrees.

People who choose to be administrators and supervisors in public schools share many of the motivations of teachers. One hope of those who become principals is that as the people in charge, they will have greater influence on a school than they have as one of many teachers. Two types of influence are obvious: what they can contribute to others and what they can achieve for themselves. Contributions to others can be expressed in terms of purposes. In surveys of middle-level and senior high school principals, the National Association of Secondary School Principals found concurrence on four of eleven possible purposes of American schools. Students should:

1. Acquire basic skills
2. Develop positive self-concepts and good human relations
3. Develop skills and practice in critical intellectual inquiry and problem solving
4. Develop moral and spiritual values

It seems reasonable to assume that, having identified these four as top priorities of American schools, principals hold these among the purposes of their own schools.

People often choose administration because it offers higher salaries and more leadership opportunities. Yet public school administrators work incredibly hard. Most work more than fifty hours a week, and it is not uncommon for them to average more than sixty hours. There are many after-school and evening obligations. Further, working conditions rarely are optimal. Too little time is available to manage the myriad administrative responsibilities, including budget, hiring, supervision, assessment, parent and student meetings, and teacher professional development. Many demands compete for an administrator's time.

CAREER PATTERNS IN EDUCATION

The common characteristics of the many professional jobs in education make it comparatively easy to move from one job to another. Certain vertical moves are typical: college professors, government and organization bureaucrats, superintendents of schools, and other top figures in education typically begin as teachers and proceed up successive rungs of a ladder in the education hierarchy.

Horizontal moves also are evident. A reading teacher may for a time teach youngsters who are gifted and talented and later shift to teaching youngsters who have learning disabilities, or a middle school teacher may after a number of years switch to a high school. On other rungs of the ladder, a director of an instructional materials center may become the head of professional development for a district or the director of a district media center. Careers in education, then, can involve vertical and horizontal moves. Numerous job shifts are possible, provided that the economy and supply and demand remain as they are or improve.

THE SCOPE OF THIS BOOK

This chapter provides an introduction to careers in education and is important as background to the whole enterprise. The person interested in any career in education should read it before reading about a particular career.

We also recommend reading Chapter 2 in its entirety, or at least the part that focuses on the act of teaching, regardless of context. Teaching is both a science and an art. Fundamental competencies have been identified and can be taught to prospective teachers. However, some aspects of teaching behavior are a function of self-understanding. Also, teaching styles may differ according to the practitioner's disposition and philosophy of education. Teaching itself calls for the performance of many roles and the orchestration of many methods. But outcomes are not entirely within the practitioner's control. Politics, policy, and economic constraints lead to many partially funded mandates that educators are expected to implement, often with inadequate resources and support. These and similar considerations are addressed in Chapter 2.

Chapter 2 also treats the subject of teaching in the K–12 domain, in public or private schools. Regular teachers at these levels typically work in classrooms, although they function in other contexts as well. The schedule and the organization of work vary by level (elementary, middle, and secondary) but are fairly well defined and quite similar across institutions within a given level.

Chapter 3 moves the context from the classroom to the school building and then to the school district, examining careers as leaders of these units—that is, as principals and superintendents. Research indicates that principals are key figures in public schooling and that, in the best of circumstances, they are the catalysts for quality and improvement at the building level. Superintendents are the chief executive officers, the top managers of school systems. They link the school to the local community and the state education agency.

In Chapter 4, attention turns to the superintendent's support staff. These are mostly behind-the-scenes people in instruction, finance and business, personnel, public relations, and other areas who keep the schools open, operating, and, ideally, advancing. Some, such as supervisors of science or home economics, oversee the content and the methods of schooling. Others manage such responsibilities as the school district's payroll, purchasing, budgeting, and accounting; its hiring, promotion, evaluation, and other personnel matters; its relations with the state and federal governments; and its relations with the local community. Still others focus on services and logistics, like plant maintenance, transportation, and food.

Chapter 5 examines the roles of the professionals who address particular aspects of young people's growth and development, such as reading skills, expressiveness, appreciation of the arts and humanities, social and psychological development, mental health, physical functioning, general welfare, educational future, and speech and hearing abilities. Examples of this type of personnel are art, music, and special education teachers; school counselors and psychologists; librarians and media specialists; nurses; occupational and physical therapists; and social workers. These specialists may work with students directly, but they also may help students indirectly, by consulting with teachers, principals, parents, and other school personnel.

Careers in two- and four-year colleges and universities are discussed in Chapter 6. In all three types of institutions, the roles of teacher and administrator are prominent. At the four-year college and university level, the roles of teacher-researcher and researcher emerge. These roles are not wholly absent in elementary and secondary schools or two-year colleges; they are simply rarities in those contexts. Roles analogous to some of the specialist positions described in Chapter 5 also are treated—for example, student affairs officers, whose responsibilities resemble those of school counselors.

Chapter 7 transports the reader from the subject of careers in traditional education to that of careers in the nontraditional realm. The focus is education that is intended to benefit the individual, be it work or leisure related. Some educators in this domain are employed in traditional institutions, and some in new delivery systems, but all are teaching, administering, or counseling in nontraditional ways—for example, in independent study and distance learning.

Chapter 8 explores careers in continuing education that are job oriented and profit motivated. Attention here is on training and development in the private sector, including efforts to keep employees abreast of technological advances, to boost their morale, and to increase their productivity. Education in this sector has long existed in the form of on-the-job training, but it has mushroomed as the country has been transformed from an industrial society to a postindustrial one grounded in information and service.

Chapter 9 focuses on the agencies, councils, and professional associations that monitor and provide technical assistance to the professionals, institutions, and organizations discussed in Chapters 2 through 7. They influence, and in some cases mandate, standards for training and, to a lesser extent, standards for practice. Many of them also have formulated ethical principles. Virtually all are involved in the accreditation of programs that prepare candidates for their field, in the recognition or approval of programs, or in the credentialing of individual practitioners.

The data in this book are the most up-to-date available at the time of writing. Nevertheless, certain kinds of data, such as those on salaries, are frequently two or three years old by the time they are published. Hence we recommend exploring the various Internet resources that are identified in the Appendix. Most agencies and associations have websites. Readers who need the most recent data can find website addresses in this appendix. The Bibliography lists relevant print materials.

Obviously, this volume does not cover every conceivable career in education. For example, it omits discussion of positions in *proprietary* (profit-making) schools at the elementary and secondary levels. It does not address short-term teaching and administration, such as overseas assignments in the Peace Corps or Department of Defense schools, or stints in colleges operated by private corporations. It makes little mention of religious education. Also, there is no attention to work in radio and television instruction, or to the administrative and other positions attendant on those activities. The book does not treat private tutoring or lessons, camp work, and athletic coaching, all of which are kinds of teaching, nor does it address preschool teaching and work in daycare centers, which are becoming prominent new areas of education.

Neglected too are education careers in the government (except in education agencies) and the military. Many programs exist. Furthermore, both the government and the military invest vast sums in training and development of civil servants and service members, analogous to the business and industry effort described in Chapter 8.

These omissions may be perceived as mistaken, but they were deliberate. Boundaries must be drawn somewhere.

FIRSTHAND ACCOUNTS

Choosing a career in education can lead a person in a number of directions. If the person is knowledgeable about the possibilities, then informed choices are easier. Ideally, making informed choices will lead to a satisfying and rewarding career in education.

What better way is there to learn about the broad field of education than to hear from some of the people who have chosen it as a career? Included throughout this book are firsthand accounts from a range of educators. Readers can review what veterans have to say, take note of their own aspirations, then draw their own conclusions.

CHAPTER 2

TEACHING IN K–12 SCHOOLS

Today, about one-third of the people choosing to become teachers do so at different ages than in the past, and they take various routes to preparing for their profession. About two-thirds prepare to teach while they are in their junior and senior years of college, but one-third or so seek preparation after earning a bachelor's degree. Many of the latter group are changing careers in their late twenties or early thirties; some are even older.

Traditionally, candidates who seek preparation after earning a bachelor's degree have enrolled in Master of Arts in Teaching programs immediately or shortly after completing their bachelor's degree. These one- or two-year university-based programs focus on teaching, offering theory and practice. In the last two decades, however, *alternative teacher education programs* have emerged in a variety of formats and with wide differences in thoroughness. These programs give candidates some education background, perhaps in a ten-week summer session, then place them in the classroom, ideally with supervision. Examples are Troops to Teachers, School-Based Teacher Education, Teach for America, Transition to Teaching Programs, and NCTeach.

A prospective teacher should select a teacher education program—undergraduate or graduate, traditional or alternative—with great care. Research on and reliable assessments of most programs are available through a number of sources, among them the ERIC Center on Teaching and Teacher Education, the American Association of Colleges for Teacher Education, the National Council for Accreditation of Teacher Education, and the Teacher Education Accreditation Council.

The changes in how people approach a career in teaching have developed primarily as a result of four conditions. First, the realities of teaching have been highly publicized (not always accurately) as education has gained greater public attention. People exploring teaching have learned that jobs vary greatly and that teaching is no simple endeavor. Particularly in urban and rural areas, it can be very difficult. A few such assignments are only for those who truly want to help disadvantaged, abused, neglected, or disillusioned youngsters and who have the temperament, the ingenuity, and the disposition to deal with them. In rural schools in remote locales or poverty zones, instructional materials, equipment, media, and facilities often are inadequate. Exposures and experiences available to students are usually minimal, and a teacher's personal life and privacy are limited. Teachers in such schools must have a strong social commitment and the skills, emotional stability, tenacity, and personality to handle the special problems that arise. Even teaching in affluent suburbs can be difficult, particularly when students have everything money can buy, but little depth or self-discipline.

Most teaching positions are challenging when the school culture is radically different from the teacher's background and experience. Teaching can yield great satisfaction in any situation if the fit between the teacher and the situation is right, but people must carefully explore the type of school and context in which they can find professional satisfaction and personal fulfillment.

A second reason that people now look differently at teaching is that employment prospects are good. A serious teacher shortage will exist for the next several years. In a number of school districts, the shortage is critical in some areas, such as special education, mathematics, and science.

Improvement in salaries is the third reason that people are considering teaching differently. Although the financial rewards of teaching are far from equal to those of many other fields requiring a college degree, substantial progress has been made in the last several years. In addition, job security and fringe benefits are much better than in most other professions.

Finally, teaching is attracting candidates who are mature. As noted earlier, about one-third of teachers in training are older—twenty-five years of age or more. A number of such candidates are entering teaching from another career. They bring a broader perspective and a greater seriousness to their career choice. They also bring richer backgrounds and greater wisdom to their practice.

The prospect of more people choosing teaching with their eyes wide open augurs well for the profession. Schools should become better places to work if they are staffed by people who select teaching after comparing it with other possibilities and taking a careful look at their own aptitudes, proclivities, and talents. The purpose of this chapter is to help readers make such an examination. Most of the chapter deals with teaching in public schools, later discussing some characteristics that differentiate private school teaching from public school teaching.

PUBLIC SCHOOL TEACHING

Teaching differs from work in industry and business. Its method, purpose, and process are distinctive in several ways. Teaching and learning, for instance, have no clear cause-and-effect relationship. No one claims with assurance that a given lesson will result in a precise learning outcome. Research confirms that children who go to school learn more than children who do not. But whether learning can be attributed directly to teachers often is uncertain. More probably, learning is the result of a complex of factors, such as socioeconomic background, innate ability, school context, socialization, and quality teaching. Also, learning often cannot be verified immediately but must be determined over time—weeks, months, and years. Many variables intervene, and learners are quite different.

Teachers, however, are not absolved of accountability. Parents and other citizens want assurances that teachers and schools are doing their job.

Teaching as a Science

In the last twenty-five years, educators have begun to define more precisely what teaching is and what a competent teacher should know and be able to do. The elements of teaching have been drawn from experience and research, and they have begun to constitute a science, or technology, of teaching. (In this context, *technology* is defined as "the means of getting a job done.") Although the development of a technology of teaching has not conclusively demonstrated that one technique is more effective than another or that good teachers can be precisely distinguished from other teachers, it has given the profession more respectability as teaching becomes more evidence-based.

The problem, however, has not been codifying the elements of teaching but ascertaining whether a given teacher has mastered essential competencies. The situation is further complicated because there are no guarantees that teachers who have demonstrated competence will exercise it day in and day out.

The elements of teaching represent what has long been taught, at least theoretically, in good teacher education programs. Lately those elements have been made more explicit in terms of teacher behavior. Some have become the basis of state evaluation systems—for example, in Connecticut, Florida, Georgia, and North Carolina. For people exploring teaching, such systems illustrate the essential elements of teaching, the legal expectations, and the official standards against which performance is evaluated for a regular teaching license and probably for tenure.

For example, the North Carolina Teacher Performance Appraisal Instrument, used for both formative and summative evaluation, identifies eight behaviors that a teacher must be able to demonstrate:

1. Manage instructional time
2. Manage student behavior
3. Present instruction
4. Monitor student performance
5. Provide instructional feedback
6. Facilitate instruction
7. Communicate within the educational environment
8. Perform noninstructional duties

During the first three years of teaching, the adequacy of a North Carolina teacher for a standard license is measured with this tool.

The National Teacher Examination, created by the Educational Testing Service, had wide use in the United States for many years. The Praxis System, initiated in 1994, has superseded it. The Praxis System consists of three tests, administered in three phases of teacher education: Praxis I, during preservice education; Praxis II, on graduation from a teacher education program; and Praxis III, after initial induction. (Praxis III is in the beginning stage of being implemented. At the time of this writing it is used in only two states.) The system relies on test results in Praxis I and II and outside evaluators in Praxis III.

But there is more to teaching than meeting standards. In many ways, teaching is imprecise work. Standard techniques to ensure that it produces learning for every student in all situations do not exist. Learning develops over time. It is seldom all or nothing. Usually it is a matter of degree. How adequately a student learns knowledge and skills in school depends on many factors, among them how well teachers diagnose motivation, ability, and attitude and how effectively they translate their diagnosis into effective teaching.

Context also is a major influence on achievement in both teaching and learning. Context is the social and psychological climate of the school, the teaching resources available, the way in which time is used, the quality of management, the physical environment, the lifestyle of the student body, the school setting, and the quality of school life.

A student's life outside school is another substantial influence on what is learned. Isolating exactly what is learned in school from what is learned elsewhere often is difficult.

Teaching as an Art

Artistry, the exercise of talents or intuition, also is a part of teaching. Teacher behavior is highly individualistic. People can learn to teach, but some personality types are more adept at teaching than others. The degree to which a personality suited to teaching can be cultivated, or intuition can be acquired, is not known. For example, why a teacher has a certain spark, projects enthusiasm, probes a question, reiterates a particular point, opts to use a personal illustration, changes pace in the middle of a lesson, compliments a particular student, discusses as well as lectures, changes an assignment, or reads to a class, cannot always be explained. Part of such teaching is intuitive. But making teaching decisions amid hundreds of cues is not merely innate talent exercised automatically. It involves perception and processing, inspiration and reflection, improvisation and studied action. A teacher may sense that a particular action is the right move to make, but in choosing that action, he or she may draw on a repertoire of learned techniques. Artistic teaching is more than talking. It is a performance. It is body language, facial expression, voice modulation, intellectual gymnastics, timing and pacing, rhythm and tone, humor and empathy, harmony and chemistry—all falling appropriately into place.

Teachers are probably best challenged when they realize how little or how much they may contribute to student growth and development. Teaching is a mind-boggling job. A teacher often does not know that he or she helped a particular student until the student returns years later to say so. Moreover, what students gain may not be knowledge of subject matter. Instead, it may be skills in thinking, the inspiration to excel, an attitude about self, or a model to emulate. Consequently, teachers are constantly faced with deciding what is most important in their teaching.

Concepts of Teaching

The most obvious component of teaching is instruction of students. That means different things to different teachers, depending on how they conceive of teaching. A person's concept of teaching influences his or her approach and activities in (and outside) the classroom. After spending hundreds of hours in schools observing and interviewing teachers, Anne Bussis, Edward Chittenden, and Marianne Amarel (in *Beyond Surface Curriculum*) characterized teaching in three ways. In the most conservative characterization, the teacher concentrated mainly on transmitting the basic skills and the facts that students were expected to learn at particular grade levels. He or she emphasized politeness, hard work, and minimal disruptions. A major concern was socializing the student "into an adult stereotype, with little regard for the student's internal experience."

The middle-range teacher was described as striving to get children "to assume responsibility for their own learning, to become more self-directed," and thus to need "less and less guidance from the teacher." The teacher's social priorities were helping students to "feel good about themselves and their abilities" and to be "happy and content in learning, and experience some sense of accomplishment."

At the third level, the teacher was concerned that children know "what they are about and why," think that through, understand it, and "interject their own purposes into an activity." In the process the teacher tried to help students develop an awareness and an acceptance of self. That is, the teacher tried to help students "recognize and differentiate their feelings and abilities and accept them as legitimate and worthwhile, . . . knowing self and experiencing self-respect in order to cope better with life."

There are many concepts of teaching because people have different philosophies of education and different beliefs about how learning takes place. It is important for teachers to know what they believe teaching to be and, for their greatest contentment, to seek employment in a school where they can practice what they believe.

The Many Roles of Teachers

Few people who explore teaching realize fully the many tasks and duties that teachers must assume in an effective school. In a small number of well-supported schools with enlightened leadership, action to recognize and support the multiple roles that teachers should take has begun. These roles may be categorized as follows:

- Individual professional
- Teacher of students
- Member of a faculty
- Member of a staff hierarchy
- Liaison with parents and the public
- Colleague of other professional educators
- Member of a teacher organization
- Member of the teaching profession

Clearly, teaching is more than what goes on for five or six hours in a single classroom. As the multiple tasks of teaching are recognized, there is a better chance that more adequate time will be allocated to all the roles that contribute to a fully functioning professional teacher.

Other Factors Influencing Teaching

Teaching practice varies greatly in terms of students, who may be diverse in ethnicity, cultural norms and values, talents, abilities and disabilities, language, socioeconomic background, and prior experience. School climate and the community in which the school is located are other influences on teaching.

The way a school is organized shapes teaching, too. For example, in schools where teachers are assigned classes of students with whom they work alone, they are solo performers. For most of the day, they do not interact with other adults. However, the value of more interchange with colleagues has gained recognition in educational thinking. The prospects are that as teachers gain greater authority in decision making, there will be more collaborating and sharing among them, much to the advantage of students. Teachers know that when teachers work together, one and one can add up to more than two.

Some middle schools have a school structure that allows for collaborative action and sharing. Teachers in language arts, mathematics, science, and social studies work as a team with a group of students. They have a common planning period each day to share teaching experiences and to exchange information on student progress across fields of study. They also have individual planning periods to shape their own teaching plans.

Still another variable in teaching is method or technique—how a teacher teaches. Several factors influence method: a teacher's knowledge of various teaching strategies, concept of teaching, and view of the purpose of education and the process of learning; facilities; equipment; the quality of administrative leadership; and the school district's goals. Making a subject come alive so that a student thinks seriously about a problem or is eager to explore a phenomenon is constantly a challenge. Teachers often are constrained by having to cover certain content in a course. Textbooks adopted by school districts may establish basic subject matter to be learned. Standardized tests also set parameters for the content and the knowledge to be taught. In some schools the emphasis on testing substantially influences what is taught. Under pressure for students to perform well on standardized tests, teachers tend to emphasize content that they know will be tested.

Variety in Teaching

Variety in teaching is considerable. There are different age groups, different subjects, and different types of students. All three distinctions are influential in shaping the nature of teaching.

Table 2.1 lists the most common categories of teachers, the types of schools in which they teach, and the kinds of teaching licenses that they must hold.

Clear differentiations in teaching are made among kindergarten, elementary school, middle and junior high school, high school, and *special-area* teachers (teachers who work in fields other than the core subjects). Usually, though, state departments of education promulgate program and licensure requirements only for elementary, secondary, and special-area teachers.

Some colleges and universities prepare prekindergarten and nursery school teachers, but in most states a license is not required or available at either level. State departments of education are beginning to recognize the importance of teaching young children and thus the need for standards and licensure for preschool teachers. A few states now license early childhood (preschool) teachers.

Middle schools are a comparatively new invention in American public education. Consequently there is not a longstanding tradition of preparation and licensure of middle school teachers. Several colleges and univer-

Table 2.1 Types of Teachers, Types of Schools, and Licenses

Type of Teacher	Type of School	License Required
Preschool	Prekindergarten or nursery school	Usually not licensed
Elementary school	Kindergarten, Grades 1–6	Early childhood license or K–6 license
Middle school	Grades 4–8, grades 5–7, grades 6–8, or grades 6–9	K–6, K–8, or secondary school teacher license[1] depending on grades encompassed in school
Junior or senior high school, core subject	Grades 6–8, grades 7–9, grades 8–9, grades 7–12, grades 9–12, or grades 10–12	K–8 or secondary school teacher license[1] (the latter endorsed in field of specialization), depending on grades encompassed in school
Special area (music, art, physical education, special education, home economics, industrial arts, or foreign language)	K–6, K–8, K–12, grades 7–12, grades 9–12, or grades 10–12	K–6, K–8, K–12, 7–12, or 9–12 license (the latter three endorsed in field of specialization), depending on grades encompassed in school

[1] Almost always with a major in a subject; sometimes also with a minor in a subject.

sities have such preparation programs, but in practice middle schools have been staffed largely by teachers trained as elementary or secondary school teachers.

Most special-area teachers are included in Table 2.1. Special education teachers, who serve *exceptional children* (children who are disabled or gifted), also are included. A few special education teachers still work all day in special rooms for students with disabilities. Often these children are not classified by grade level. Other special education teachers work for part of the day with students, who rotate between regular classrooms and special education, and for the other part of the day with regular teachers. The practice of *inclusion*—placing exceptional children in regular classrooms—is changing the role of most special education teachers. They are becoming consultants to, or coteachers with, regular classroom teachers. Special education teachers and other special-area teachers, such as specialists in reading and speech correction, are discussed in Chapter 5, along with school counselors, school psychologists, nurses, social workers, and other special service personnel.

Political Influences on Teaching and Schooling

Following the launch of *Sputnik* in 1957, political, industrial, and military leaders, as well as citizens across the country, became highly concerned about the adequacy and quality of American education. The resulting efforts have not affected teachers directly, but they have gradually changed a number of the nation's educational goals and policies. Perhaps most important, they have drawn attention to the importance of education.

A fairly recent example occurred in 1989. At the invitation of President George H. W. Bush, the governors of the fifty states met to discuss the condition of American education. They agreed on six national goals to guide the improvement of education, including having all children starting school ready to learn and increasing the high school graduation rate to 90 percent. The goals were discussed across the country and became generally accepted as targets for revitalizing schooling. Through a national goals panel, the public, state legislators, and boards of education became more active in promoting education. In 1994, with support from the Clinton administration, two goals were added to the original six, and all eight were sanctioned in a law called Goals 2000: The Educate America Act.

These goals were superseded by new federal legislation in 2002, called the No Child Left Behind Act. This legislation, proposed by the administration of George W. Bush with congressional support, stated its mission in six goals:

1. Create a culture of achievement
2. Improve student achievement
3. Develop safe schools and strong character
4. Transform education into an evidence-based field
5. Enhance the quality of and access to postsecondary and adult education
6. Establish management excellence

Most citizens would endorse these goals. The program specifications and requirements, however, may elicit a mixed reaction. They make obvious a more directive agenda and flavor: for example, an objective that all students read on grade level by the third grade; more federal oversight; and a narrower focus on education, especially prekindergarten through grade 12.

Some provisions of the No Child Left Behind Act, for states that participate, are as follows:

- Assessment of students in mathematics, reading, and science (no other subjects)
- Participation in the National Assessment of Educational Progress
- Development of standards for adequate yearly progress, with all students to reach proficiency or an advanced level of achievement within twelve years
- Adherence to a sequence of consequences (such as *school choice*— that is, allowing parents to choose to send their children elsewhere in the public school system, or to private schools) for schools that fail to meet the standards for adequate yearly progress for two or more consecutive years
- Modification of formulas for allocating funds, in order to target high-poverty districts
- Assurance that teachers meet the act's definition of "highly qualified" by the end of the 2005–06 school year
- Expansion of federal support for school choice

How these provisions will be carried out is yet to be determined. Implementation of the act requires a great deal of paperwork for local districts, state departments of education, and colleges and universities. In addition, definitions of phrases like *adequate yearly progress* and *highly qualified teachers* are not in the legislation and must be developed.

The act takes a carrot-and-stick approach; that is, to be eligible to receive federal funds, states must follow the act's directives. At this writing, only two states have decided not to participate. A contradiction between the legislation and the U.S. Constitution is that the latter assigns responsibility for education to the states, yet the legislation prescribes what the states should do. Of course, participation is voluntary.

The Magnitude of Public Education

The public school enterprise is enormous. It serves more than 47 million students and employs more than 3.7 million teachers. Each grade in public schools enrolls more than 3.5 million students, except for grades 11 and 12, which enroll about 3 million each. In fall 2002 there were 28.4 million children in grades 1 through 8 and 13.5 million youngsters in grades 9 through 12, plus more than 0.4 million children in preschool and kindergarten. More than 5 million students (newborn to twenty-one years of age) are served by programs for youngsters with disabilities, funded by the Individuals with Disabilities Education Act and Chapter 1 of the Education Consolidation and Improvement Act.

Estimates are that retirements alone will create a need for 2.4 million additional teachers in the next decade. However, demand will differ by state and region. Mountain and Pacific states are projected to increase enrollment by at least 20 percent, some by as much as 50 percent.

The Work Schedule

The typical instructional day for students is five to five-and-a-half hours long, Monday through Friday. In some other countries, schools also are in session on Saturday. Several national commissions and committees studying American education have recommended longer school days and more school days per year in the United States. Kindergarten students usually spend half a day in school, although some school districts have moved to all-day kindergarten. Students in grades 1 through 6 (elementary schools) attend school all day and usually are taught by one teacher for most of the day. Teachers of art, music, and physical education in the elementary school often teach their subject two or three times a week in all grades, either in the students' regular classroom or in a room especially designed for their field—an art room, a music room, or a gymnasium. In some schools, classroom teachers teach all the subjects, and special-area teachers serve as consultants to, or team-teach with, classroom teachers.

Middle schools (typically encompassing grades 4 through 6 or 6 through 8) are organized in several ways. A popular model, noted earlier, assembles faculty into teams consisting of one teacher from each of the core subjects (language arts, mathematics, science, and social studies). Each team works with a cadre of about 100 students. Team members have a common period each day for planning. Although students move from class to class for each subject, they often are in their own wing of a building for core subjects. For other subjects—art, home economics, industrial arts, music, and physical education—they go to special teachers.

Junior high schools almost always are departmentalized. Teachers remain in the same classroom throughout the day, and students come to them in groups or sections. They teach five or six sections each day, a new one every 45 to 55 minutes. In addition, they manage a homeroom, where students assemble each morning and return in the afternoon. To an extent the homeroom provides a guidance function: the teacher gets to know students individually and remains with them for a full school year.

Some junior high schools use large blocks of time for English and social studies. Some block programs are labeled *core curriculum*. That is, English and social studies are taught in an integrated mode, and the teacher also serves in a guidance capacity similar to that of a homeroom teacher. The core curriculum seems to ebb and flow in popularity. Where public school programs have become more conservative in philosophy, the focus is more on a separate course for each subject.

Special-area teachers in such fields as computer science, foreign languages, health, home economics, and industrial arts join with those in art, music, and physical education to provide a broader program of studies in many middle and junior high schools. In some schools, though, the arts are receiving less emphasis; indeed, in places they are almost nonexistent. School counselors, school psychologists, assistant principals, attendance officers, and coaches fill out the instructional staff in many middle and junior high schools. Some teach and some do not, but all have contact with both teachers and students.

Almost all senior high schools are organized into departments by subject. The exceptions are alternative and progressive high schools, where both teachers and subjects may be integrated, and magnet schools, where a particular area of study, such as science and technology or music and art, is the emphasis. Departments in the typical high school vary in size. English, mathematics, science, and social studies departments (in that order) are the largest because several years of those subjects are required.

The Organization of Work

Teaching in K–12 schools most often takes place in classes. Typically the teacher instructs the whole class for the entire period. In other patterns, teachers instruct the whole class some of the time but also have students work independently and in small groups. In English or language arts, for example, students may critique one another's written work or engage in discussion and debate. In science they may take part in hands-on projects and experiments, individually and in groups. In social studies they may participate in learning games and mock situations, and engage in debates, discussions, and problem solving. The teacher is centrally involved in planning and managing such activities. The multitude of organizational schemes that teachers devise all are designed to help students learn.

Teachers must provide for different interests, motivations, and abilities. This creates tension, as educational sociologist Ronald G. Corwin points out:

> Because students are in groups, the particular immaturities of some children may force procedures on all that prove alienating. For example, to maintain order, a teacher may be forced to become more austere than she wishes to be. This tension between "discipline" and instilling confidence and enthusiasm among students is one of the basic challenges of working with energetic young people.

The elementary school teacher must find ways to individualize instruction, often while faced with twenty-five children in a daylong schedule. Some teachers use *learning centers*, which allow students to work in smaller groups in different areas of emphasis. Middle, junior high, and senior high school teachers must try to attend to individual differences as they teach four or five classes, with more than 100 students each day.

In addition, teachers plan lessons and activities, read and critique student work, serve on committees, monitor lunches and recess, perform bus duty, advise extracurricular activities, meet with parents, and take part in school-sponsored professional development sessions.

Current Reform Efforts

Current efforts to reform schools include various attempts to reduce overloads and excesses. The goals are to help teachers increase the quantity and improve the quality of learning and to serve individual students better. Unfortunately, there is a long way to go to reach these goals. New teachers join an army of educators who want tomorrow to be better than yesterday but are not always sure how to make that happen in a large bureaucracy. Contemporary recommendations that teachers be given greater authority to make instructional decisions could improve both teaching and the lives of students.

More Personnel in the Classroom

The use of more than one adult to work with a class of students has been a gradual development. As yet, only a few schools embrace the practice, but it will grow as teachers become more comfortable with it and as parents and teachers recognize how much more can be accomplished by it.

Teacher aides (or assistants) are one type of personnel being added. In some states all teachers in the first three grades have an aide. Evidence indicates that instruction improves if an assistant is available to free the teacher from some of the paperwork and other day-to-day details of the job. Teacher aides assist in preparation and use of instructional materials, preparation of the classroom (for example, setting up desks and chairs and creating bulletin boards), creation of the classroom environment (for example, arranging learning centers and supporting cooperative learning), instruction, and performance of lunchroom and playground duty.

Another approach that employs more than one adult in a class is team-teaching, or cooperative teaching. Two or more teachers work together or in turns in a class. When more than one professional is present to work with a class and with individuals, the perception, the understanding, and the knowledge put into teaching are at least doubled. Conferring regularly with another professional provides teachers with relief and support in a job that inundates them. The presence of more personnel also makes additional guidance available and provides students with more options regarding whom they might consult. Students can choose to work with the teacher with whom they feel more comfortable.

More Kinds of Personnel Involved in Schools

Two kinds of innovative programs under way around the country assemble even more professionals to address the growth and development of children, youth, and families. The professional development school, a collaboration between a school and a college or university, expands the school staff to include college professors, interns and student teachers, researchers, teacher aides, volunteers, parents, and others. This kind of school, often compared with a teaching hospital, is designed to serve K–12 students, to provide supervised experience for prospective teachers, to support research and experimentation in schools, and to demonstrate promising practices.

An extension of the professional development school is the interprofessional development school, which uses not only educators but personnel from other human services—social workers, psychologists, child care workers, nurses, physicians, other health professionals, tutors, mentors from business and industry, adult literacy specialists, and more—to serve the multiple needs of children and families. Some herald the interprofessional development school as the successor to the traditional school—a family-centered, community-based collaborative that integrates various components of human service. At least 100 interprofessional development schools are in existence today. (For more information, see Chapter 6 of *Teachers for the New Millennium*, edited by Leonard Kaplan and Roy A. Edelfelt.)

Mentoring

To help new teachers, a number of schools have begun mentor programs, often financed by the state. Selected experienced teachers, many of them with special training, assist beginners in the first year or two. Often called *mentors*, these teachers serve in an advisory rather than a supervisory role. They do not evaluate beginners for job retention. Rather, they help beginners with such problems as preparing lessons, finding materials, organizing time, managing discipline, and individualizing instruction. Also, they provide confidential feedback on teaching performance.

Help for the career teacher has been slower to develop and more difficult to bring about because experience usually establishes habits and routines that are hard to break. Also, seasoned professionals often have difficulty admitting that long-used practices and procedures could be improved or might be outdated. Assisting career teachers is more effective when it happens at the request of the veteran. That has happened in a few instances when the school climate is right and the work of mentors for beginning teachers has been so successful that regular teachers seek out mentors for help.

Reduction of Class Size

Progress has been made in reducing class size, which tends to improve student learning. In 1999–2000, classes in elementary schools averaged 21.2 children; in departmentalized secondary schools, 23.4 youngsters.

Change of Assignment

Another approach to stimulating and revitalizing teachers is to encourage them to change assignments. For example, a third-grade teacher might switch to fifth grade, or a teacher of senior English might teach sophomores. The idea seems to work best when it originates with the teacher or at least is implemented with his or her concurrence.

Other Approaches

Among other efforts to break with tradition and seek more effective ways to teach are career ladder programs and use of lead teachers. *Career ladder programs* are arrangements that allow paraprofessional personnel (teacher assistants, teacher aides, and the like) to step gradually into the role of licensed teacher, as one might do in a work-study program. *Lead teachers* are highly competent, experienced teachers in charge of a team of teachers in various arrangements of staffing. One such arrangement is *differentiated staffing*, in which teachers take different roles and responsibilities depending on their level of skill or specialty, and are paid accordingly.

A growing number of school districts have given teachers more latitude in decision making—for example, a greater voice in curriculum and teaching and a voice in hiring, promotion, instruction, and budget decisions.

Having greater control of their destiny has been a goal of teachers for many years. In the late 1990s, recommendations to that effect by national panels and commissions held new promise of implementation.

Adequate Budget

Few of these ideas and goals are new, but there has been a fresh commitment to implement them. An adequate budget is essential, however. Congress appropriated $53.1 billion in discretionary funding for the U.S. Department of Education for fiscal year 2002–03. That represented a 6.4 percent increase over fiscal year 2001–02. In 2003, though, most states found themselves in dire financial circumstances, making the prospect of substantial increases in state budgets for education questionable.

Preparation

States have regulated entry into the teaching profession for more than 100 years, initially through the issuance of licenses to teach in the public schools and subsequently also through the approval of college and university programs for teacher preparation. Since the turn of the century, requirements for teacher preparation and licensure have been steadily upgraded, with those for secondary education setting the pace (see Table 2.2). All fifty states now require public school teachers to hold a valid state license issued by the state's office of teacher education and certification or a professional standards board. In most cases a state department or standards board issues an initial license on the basis of a recommendation from the college at which the candidate earned his or her degree (in a program approved by the state department or standards board). A bachelor's degree that includes courses in foundations of education and pedagogy, and a stint as a student teacher or an intern, are universally required for the initial license. The experience as a student teacher or an intern must be supervised by a university professor and an experienced schoolteacher.

The trend has been for states to require more than an initial license. Teachers usually must earn a regular or standard license within a few years after receiving their initial license. As of 2003, forty-one states offered a second-stage license, although only twenty-seven of them required it. Requirements for the regular license vary, usually including a master's degree, a specified number of hours of graduate study or units of contin-

Table 2.2 Growth of the United States, Education, and Teacher Education, 1869–2000

School Year	Num-ber of States	Public School Enrollment				Number of Institutions Preparing Teachers			Number of States Requiring Bachelor's Degree for Certification	
		U.S. Population	Elementary School	Secondary School	Number of Public School Teachers	Normal Schools	Teachers Colleges	Total Institutions Preparing Teachers	Elemen-tary School Teachers	Second-ary School Teachers
1869–1870	37	39,818,000	6,792,000	80,000	201,000	69	0	78	0	0
1879–1880	38	50,156,000	9,757,000	110,000	287,000	ND	0	ND	0	0
1889–1890	44	62,948,000	12,520,000	203,000	364,000	204	0	234	0	0
1899–1900	45	75,995,000	14,984,000	519,000	423,000	289	2	ND	0	2
1909–1910	46	90,490,000	16,899,000	915,000	523,000	247	12	379	0	3
1919–1920	48	104,514,000	19,378,000	2,200,000	657,000	326	46	ND	0	10[1]
1929–1930	48	121,767,000	21,279,000	4,399,000	843,000	212	134	839	2[1]	23
1939–1940	48	130,879,718	18,833,000	6,601,000	875,000	103	186	ND	11	40
1949–1950	48	149,188,130	19,387,000	5,725,000	914,000	5	138	1,005	21	42[2]
1959–1960	50	177,829,628	27,602,000	8,485,000	1,387,000	0	55	1,150	39	51
1969–1970	50	202,676,946	32,597,000	13,022,000	2,131,000	0	16	1,246	47	52
1979–1980	50	225,055,487	27,931,000	13,714,000	2,300,000	0	10	1,365	52[2]	52
1989–1990	50	246,819,230	29,152,000	11,390,000	2,860,000	0	0	ND	52	52
1999–2000	50	272,690,813	33,488,158	13,369,163	2,907,000	0	0	1,417	52	52

ND = No data

[1] The District of Columbia is included in this figure and the following figures in this column.
[2] Puerto Rico is included in this figure and the following figures in this column.

Sources: From *Digest of Education Statistics 1995*, by T. D. Snyder, 1995, Washington, DC: National Center for Education Statistics; *Mini-Digest of Education Statistics 2001*, by National Center for Education Statistics, 2002, Washington, DC: Author; *A Manual on Standards Affecting*

continued

Table 2.2 *continued*

School Personnel in the United States, edited by T. M. Stinnett, 1974, Washington, DC: National Education Association; *The NASDTEC Manual on Preparation and Certification of Educational Personnel for the Year 2002* (7th ed.), by National Association of State Directors of Teacher Education and Certification, 2002, Dubuque, IA: Kendall/Hunt; *National Survey of the Education of Teachers,* Vol. 6, *Special Survey Studies,* by B. W. Frazier, G. L. Betts, W. J. Greenleaf, D. Waples, N. H. Dearborn, M. Carney, and T. Alexander, 1935, Washington, DC: U.S. Government Printing Office; *Projections of Education Statistics to 2006* (25th ed.), edited by W. J. Hussar and D. E. Gerald, 1996, Washington, DC: National Center for Education Statistics; and *A Study of Teacher Education Institutions as Innovators, Knowledge Producers, and Change Agents,* by D. L. Clark and E. G. Guba, 1977, Bloomington, IN: Indiana University.

uing education, three or more years of experience, and a performance assessment. Some states require teachers to extend or renew the standard license periodically, usually by completing a certain number of graduate credit hours or professional development units every year.

In some states, licenses are generic for teaching but endorsed for a certain level (such as elementary or secondary school), subject (such as English or mathematics), or special area (such as home economics, industrial arts, or special education). In other states, licenses are for elementary or secondary school teaching or certain special areas, and there may be endorsements for subjects (such as English or social studies) and other special areas (such as art, music, and physical education). The license for middle school teaching is separate in a few states, included in a junior high school license in most other states.

All the teacher education programs that a college or university offers must be approved by the state department of education or a professional standards board. On the strength of such approval, many state departments of education or standards boards now issue licenses to graduates of approved programs, provided that the college recommends the graduates.

All the licenses or certifications just discussed are required by the states. In addition, in 1993 a national professional certification was established in twenty-six areas or levels of teaching. This advanced certification is comparable to the diplomate in other professions. National certification is governed by the National Board for Professional Teaching Standards, a nonprofit body made up of teachers, subject matter specialists from schools and colleges, and other professional educators. Application for national certification is voluntary for teachers with three or more years of experience. Teachers who successfully complete the national certification process are usually recognized by their district or state with salary increases. As of 2002, more than 16,000 teachers had achieved this distinction.

Teacher education programs also are monitored by both regional and national accreditation. Both of these processes are voluntary; that is, institutions choose whether to be reviewed. Across the country there are six regional accrediting associations. Their focus is the general quality of a college or university. At the national level, two agencies accredit programs that prepare teachers and other education personnel: the National Council for Accreditation of Teacher Education (NCATE) and the Teacher Education Accreditation Council (TEAC). NCATE accredits programs against standards that it has developed. Its constituent organizations represent public school teachers, education and subject matter professionals, and colleges of teacher education. Accreditation by NCATE involves, first, an institution preparing a report that explains how its program conforms to NCATE's standards; then, a cross-section of educators from outside the state conducting a site visit to validate that the standards have been met.

TEAC bases accreditation on an audit of the adequacy of evidence that faculty present to demonstrate three basic principles of quality: evidence of student learning, evidence that the assessment of student learning is valid, and evidence of the program's continuous improvement and quality control. TEAC requires faculty members of a program applying for accreditation to submit an *inquiry brief*, a research monograph in which they present the evidence supporting their claim that their program satisfies the three basic principles. Auditors then visit the institution to verify the accuracy of the evidence in the inquiry brief.

A prospective teacher should check the accreditation status of the colleges and programs he or she is considering.

Standard preparation programs vary somewhat for elementary, secondary, and special education teachers, but all candidates must take courses in general education, subject matter, and pedagogical studies. They also must study human growth and development, with an emphasis on children or adolescents, depending on the level at which they expect to teach. Most programs require clinical experiences in schools before admission to student teaching or an internship. In all states, programs require student teaching or a full-time internship for eight to eighteen weeks, supervised by both schoolteachers and college professors. A 1996 report by the National Commission on Teaching and America's Future recommends yearlong internships in professional development schools to "allow extended practice in teaching in schools tightly tied to relevant coursework." Implementation of this recommendation is under way in a few programs.

Almost all states require prospective middle, junior high, and high school teachers to complete courses in social and philosophical foundations of education and the nature of student learning and development. Also required are a program of liberal studies (general education), a major in the candidate's teaching field, and instruction in pedagogy and methods of teaching the major subject. In some states, candidates also must have a minor in the second subject or area they will teach.

Prospective elementary school teachers are prepared to teach all the subjects of the K–6 curriculum. They also are required to complete a program of liberal studies. In some states this involves concentrations in the major subjects taught in the elementary school, or a major in a subject field. Further, they must receive instruction in pedagogy and methods of teaching the subjects of the elementary school.

Art, music, physical education, and special education teachers focus on their specialty, but they too are required to complete courses in foundations of education, student learning and development, and pedagogy. They may have a concentration within their special field. For example, an art teacher may concentrate on painting or sculpting, a music teacher on instrumental or vocal music, a physical education teacher on sports or dance, and a special education teacher on children with hearing impairments. In several of these specialties, teachers receive preparation and are licensed to teach students from kindergarten through grade 12.

Career Patterns

Few good measures of the length of a typical teaching career exist. In fact, a "typical teaching career" may not exist. Some people enter teaching and stay a short time. Highly publicized data suggest that half of new teachers leave their initial position by the fifth year. Few studies have explored the reasons why teachers leave a position, so it is difficult to know what proportion actually exit the profession. In a 1991–92 study (the latest available), the National Center for Education Statistics found 87.6 percent of public school teachers to be *stayers* (teachers who stayed in the same school from the 1990–91 school year to the 1991–92 school year), 7.3 percent to be *movers* (teachers who changed schools during that period), and 5.1 percent to be leavers (teachers who left the profession). The largest group of *leavers*, 30.4 percent, retired. The next-largest group, a distant 10.9 percent, left because of pregnancy or childrearing, and the third-largest group, 10 percent, left because of a family or personal move. Frequently, leavers in both the latter groups return to teaching: those in the first group after their youngsters reach school age, those in the second after they have settled in at their new location. Another 9.8 percent departed because of school staffing actions (reductions in force, reorganizations, transfers, and the like), and 8.4 percent left to continue their education— to take courses to improve their opportunities in education or to take a sabbatical. Family and personal reasons accounted for 5.7 percent, health for 3.7 percent, better salaries and benefits for 3.6 percent, and enrollment in courses to improve opportunities for employment outside education 1.5 percent. Only 8.3 percent left because they were dissatisfied with teaching, and 7.8 percent because they wanted to pursue another career.

The study is helpful in understanding attrition in teaching, but it is not certain that these patterns continue today. The number of teachers retiring in a given year, for example, will vary depending on the age spread of the teaching force or the age or time in teaching at which a state will begin a pension.

Teaching can be a prelude to a variety of other jobs in education and in other professions. In fact, teaching fosters upward social mobility. Many people become middle class by virtue of the college education they receive to become teachers. For some, that acculturation stimulates a desire to remain in teaching or another field of education, as well as to stay where there is continuous opportunity to learn and grow. For example, almost all principals, school superintendents, and government employees in state and national education departments began their careers as teachers. Teaching exposes a person to a wide variety of new occupations and professions. Because teaching involves skills in working with people, it provides training that is appropriate, with only slight additions and modifications, for many service occupations.

Teaching has recently become a popular second career. As noted earlier, many colleges report that one-third of their teacher education students are older than the usual eighteen- to twenty-four-year-old student. People entering teaching at an older age tend to have stronger convictions about working with young people, often from experience as parents. The work schedule and the lifestyle of teaching also attract second-career people.

Finding Employment

Both new and experienced teachers can usually find assistance in job placement through the college or university they graduated from. Most teacher education institutions provide placement services that list vacancies. The more advanced the placement office, the broader the geographical spread of the jobs listed. Teachers seeking employment through a placement office must take the initiative in opening a placement file. The service is free or costs little. Placement officers provide information and counsel without charge to teachers who seek their advice.

Candidates for positions must complete a placement folder and seek recommendations for their file. The usual procedure for the candidate is to seek several professional recommendations and a few character references from people who know the candidate well. Candidates quite naturally select people who will make positive comments about them. However, the most desirable recommendations are objective and candid, not effusively complimentary. They describe the teacher's abilities, traits, temperament, and character in straightforward language and may identify a few areas of needed growth. Helpful, too, is the recommendation that gives an opinion about the kind of situation in which the candidate will be most successful. The candidate is well advised to recommend to those who write letters of support that they be candid and explicit. Most often the candidate does not see the written recommendation he or she has solicited. That encourages frank and honest opinions.

Some teacher education programs now require prospective teachers to maintain a portfolio, particularly during the professional part of their college work. Portfolios are used for both documentation and assessment. They include specimens of work, descriptions of experience, photographs, videotapes of teaching episodes, units taught during student teaching or internship, a statement of philosophy, critiques by college supervisors and cooperating teachers, and so forth. Such documentation conveys more comprehensive information to a potential employer than a standard résumé does.

Teachers also find employment by direct contact with prospective employers and through placement services offered by state education departments, teachers' unions, and private agencies. The latter charge a fee, usually a percentage of the first-year salary. Often the employing district will cover that fee if the candidate negotiates coverage before signing a contract. Placement services operated by state education departments and teachers' unions are typically low cost or free. References, once acquired, can be used for these placement files, as can other professional data.

Teachers also can contact employers on their own. Most job seekers mail copies of their résumé to several school districts where positions might be open and where they might like to teach.

Student teaching and internships provide another point of entry. The extended period that a student teacher spends in a school provides administrators, particularly principals, with opportunities to observe him or her firsthand in the classroom and to seek the opinion of cooperating teachers and the college supervisor on his or her potential. With student teaching and internships now a full-time stint of eight to eighteen weeks, the principal also can observe how the prospective teacher relates to other faculty and to parents. Naturally, when jobs open, student teachers, interns, substitute teachers, and teacher aides (with teaching credentials) of proven ability have an advantage over other applicants.

Whichever approach a teacher uses, a placement file at the college or university from which he or she graduated is advisable. It provides a central point of information for prospective employers, no matter how they may discover a candidate.

Intangible Rewards

In comparison with other people who have a similar level of education, teachers do not command high salaries. The profession offers other kinds of rewards, however, and many teachers find satisfactions that money cannot buy. One is public esteem. Parents, for example, think well of schools and, by implication, of teachers. In the 2002 Phi Delta Kappa/Gallup poll of the public's attitudes toward the public schools, a random sample of adults were asked to grade the schools locally and nationally. The choices were A, B, C, D, or FAIL. Twenty-seven percent of parents gave the school their oldest child attended an A, 44 percent a B, 20 percent a C, 6 percent a D, and 2 percent a FAIL; 1 percent did not know what grade to give.

Teachers value other rewards at least as highly as money. In an exhaustive study, an educational sociologist concluded that teachers viewed a wide range of incentives and rewards as reasons to choose and remain in teaching, money being not necessarily the most important. In another study, teachers were polled on the reasons they entered teaching and continued to teach. Responses to both questions yielded three top reasons: a desire to work with young people, the value or the significance of education in society, and job security, in that order.

Salary and Fringe Benefits

Salary and other material rewards for teaching are important if teachers are to enjoy a lifestyle that enables them to remain current, vital, and conversant with the culture they are charged to reflect, understand, and transmit. Table 2.3 compares the average hourly wages in teaching with those in selected other professions whose members are college graduates.

Teachers receive compensations other than cash. Chief among them are support for professional development and graduate study, various types of insurance, contributions toward their retirement, and leave.

Table 2.3 Average Hourly Wages of Selected Professionals in Full-Time Employment, 2001

Field	Average Hourly Wage (Dollars)
Chemists, except biochemists	31.95
Executives, administrators, managers	31.82
Engineers, architects, surveyors	31.20
Mathematical and computer scientists	30.54
Economists	29.63
Teachers, except college and university	28.49
Accountants	21.73

Source: Adapted from *National Compensation Survey, Occupational Wages in the United States, 2001*, by U.S. Department of Labor, Bureau of Labor Statistics, 2002, August, available at bls.gov/ncs/ocs/sp/ncbl0449.pdf (last visited February 23, 2003).

Teachers participate in professional development (such as conferences and institutes) and graduate study. They also attend workshops sponsored by their school districts during the school year. A significant percentage of the nation's school districts provide reimbursement for part or all of such activity.

Almost 60 percent of all teachers in 1999–2000 participated in professional development in the content of their main teaching field, and more than 70 percent participated in activities directed at the use of computers for instruction. With more teachers holding master's degrees or six-year diplomas, fewer teachers over the age of forty are electing formal graduate study. Teachers holding master's degrees have all the academic credentials required by state certification offices. Many therefore undertake a wide variety of other growth activities beyond the master's degree, including travel, conference and workshop attendance, sabbatical leaves, and special projects.

Insurance Benefits

School districts provide various types of insurance for teachers. Almost all offer hospitalization, medical/surgical, and major medical insurance. Table 2.4 presents relevant data. Among the districts providing insurance of any kind, some pay all the premiums for coverage of the employee, and a smaller number pay all the premiums for coverage of the whole family.

The insurance benefits of teachers have continued to improve, and they are much better than those of American employees across all jobs. For example, in 2000 essentially all public school teachers had health insurance, compared with 62 percent of professional and technical employees. Further, more than 80 percent had dental care coverage, whereas only 42 percent of professional and technical employees had such insurance.

A critical shortcoming of some insurance benefits, such as hospitalization and major medical insurance, is that they are not transferable from one state to another. Experienced teachers who are looking at possible employment outside their current state should inquire about the effective beginning date of hospitalization and major medical coverage. Often they can negotiate such coverage more easily before signing a contract than afterward.

Table 2.4 Insurance Benefits Provided for Teachers by School Districts

	Districts Providing (%)	Premiums Fully Paid for Employee (%)	Premiums Fully Paid for Family (%)
Hospitalization coverage	96.5	84.2	29.3
Medical/surgical coverage	95.2	84.1	29.4
Major medical coverage	95.6	84.5	28.9
Dental care coverage	80.9	85.7	36.4
Vision care coverage	48.3	82.1	41.0
Prescription drugs coverage	84.6	83.2	29.4
Group life insurance	73.3	——(varies greatly)——	
Professional liability insurance	64.5	ND	NA

ND = no data; NA = not applicable.

Source: From *Fringe Benefits for Teachers in Public Schools, 1994–95*, by Educational Research Service, 1995, Arlington, VA: Author. These are the most recent data available. In a telephone conversation in January 2003, an Educational Research Service manager said that the organization has not conducted a more recent study of these benefits because they tend not to change rapidly.

Retirement Programs

Participation in a retirement system is obligatory for almost all public school teachers, whereas only about 48 percent of the total workforce has a retirement provision. In 2002–03, 76 percent of school districts provided teacher retirement benefits under a statewide teachers' retirement system, 26 percent under a state employees' retirement system. (The two percentages add up to more than 100 because some districts reported more than one type of retirement provision.) No teachers were outside any system.

In many instances both the teacher and the school district contribute to retirement. The respective percentages of contribution vary by state and school district. Some state retirement systems are quite good, with the employer providing for a substantial contribution, which becomes the employee's property, or is *vested*, after a relatively short period (for example, five years).

Like some insurance benefits, teacher retirement provisions do not transfer from state to state. Many states, though, allow teachers to transfer years of service or buy in to a state retirement plan on the basis of experience elsewhere. Teachers moving to new employment in another state should investigate the number of years that can be credited toward retirement. As with hospitalization and medical coverage, retirement credit often is easier for teachers to negotiate before signing a contract than afterward.

Leave Provisions

Leave policies are usually determined by local school systems. According to data from the Educational Research Service, considerable variation exists in the extent of coverage and the percentage of districts granting various types of leave. For example, sick leave is granted by 99 percent of districts, but differences exist in the number of days provided, the number of days credited per year, and the number of days that can be accumulated. Family, personal/emergency, bereavement, and jury leaves are granted almost universally by districts. Substantial proportions of districts allow for professional (91 percent), military (89 percent), religious (69 percent), and sabbatical (69 percent) leaves.

PRIVATE SCHOOL TEACHING

About 404,000 teachers (full-time equivalents) teach roughly 5.3 million students (10 percent of American schoolchildren) in about 27,000 private or independent schools. Among the teachers, 37.6 percent are employed in Catholic schools, 37.9 percent in other religious schools, and 24.5 percent in nonsectarian schools.

Sixty-two percent of private school teachers hold a bachelor's degree, 30 percent a master's degree or higher. Six percent have less than a bachelor's degree.

Great diversity exists among private schools, but most have the following characteristics in common:

1. They are not controlled by the government.
2. They are primarily supported by private funds.

3. Most have some requirements for admission. (Of those that include grades 10, 11, or 12, 64.4 percent require an interview.)

4. Enrollment in them is a matter of choice.

5. They are smaller than most public schools. Only 19 percent enroll 300 or more students, compared with 69 percent of public schools.

6. They are nonprofit and tax exempt.

7. They welcome gifts and grants, and many seek such funds.

8. They select their own teachers and administrators.

9. Tuition often is their main source of revenue.

10. Except for some parochial schools, they are controlled by a local board and establish their own curriculum.

About 1,500 private schools are members of the National Association of Independent Schools (NAIS), an organization highly regarded for its attention to standards of private school education. Some 340 NAIS schools are residential (boarding); the balance are day schools.

Currently, church-related schools (mostly day schools) constitute the largest proportion of private schools—79 percent, or 21,370 schools. Of these, about 8,100 are Catholic. They enroll about 58 percent of all students attending religiously oriented schools, almost 49 percent of all students attending private schools. Nonsectarian schools make up the balance of private schools—21.5 percent, or about 5,850. They serve almost 850,000 students.

About half of the private schools operating today have developed in the last thirty-five years. These include most Hebrew schools, evangelical Lutheran schools, member schools of the Association of Christian Schools International, special education schools, and Montessori schools.

People interested in teaching in private schools should explore the accreditation status and the membership affiliation of the school that advertises employment. Inquiries at NAIS, the Council for American Private Education, the Association of Christian Schools International, and the American Association of Christian Schools will yield reliable information. Further, checking whether accreditation by the latter two organizations is recognized by the appropriate regional accrediting association is worthwhile.

In many church-related day schools, teaching conditions and approaches are much the same as in public schools. The main difference is the inclusion of religion in the curriculum. However, in a number of private schools, usually nonsectarian ones, the schedule of the school day is different, with classes in core subjects in the morning and the early afternoon, and extended periods in the mid to late afternoon for activities and study that require more than the usual one-hour class.

Most NAIS schools espouse a liberal, humanistic philosophy of education that is not unlike the progressive credo of public school teachers. That is, they advocate building a sense of community in school, providing teachers with an opportunity "to develop and shape courses and curriculum," and giving teachers "the chance to have an effect on the total development of young people." They subscribe to having teachers be "role models, advisors, and counselors." Further, they seek teachers who "have a genuine interest in and commitment to all aspects of children's growth."

Preparation

Almost 40 percent of private schools require teachers to have state certification, graduation from a state-approved teacher preparation program, and a major or minor in the field to be taught. Preparation for private school teaching is fairly similar to that for public school teaching, except that private schools do not uniformly require teachers to have training in education. A small number do not require even a bachelor's degree.

A look at the educational backgrounds of private school teachers confirms the preceding statements. Overall, about two-fifths are licensed in the field of their main assignment. There are many variations, however. About two-thirds in Catholic schools and special education schools are licensed in their main field. In all other private schools, the proportion ranges from about one-twentieth to about three-fifths.

Private school teachers in most states are not subject to state licensure requirements. The few exceptions are Hawaii, Idaho, Iowa, Michigan, and North Dakota, which require all private school teachers to be licensed.

Finding Employment

All the approaches to finding employment followed by public school teachers are appropriate for private school teachers. Placement services often are an event at national conferences of private school associations. For example, NAIS runs an employment information exchange at its national conference, at which both prospective teachers and interested employers register, and candidates and school representatives have interviews. In addition, internships, teaching fellowships, or apprentice programs are available in a number of private schools. Many pay participants, some charge participants a fee (which may be in addition to pay), and several offer possibilities for earning college credit toward licensure or a degree. NAIS maintains a roster of such opportunities in its member schools.

Salary and Fringe Benefits

The intangible rewards of private school teachers are much the same as those of public school teachers. In addition, in parochial schools, teachers with strong religious commitments may gain satisfaction from the moral and spiritual environment in which they work and the guidance that they provide. Some private school teachers would argue that the intellectual climate and the stimulating interaction with well-educated colleagues are incentives. Testimonials of independent school teachers highlight the rewards of working with young people.

Salaries typically are lower in private schools than in public schools. In 1999–2000 the average beginning salary in all private schools for teachers with a bachelor's degree and no experience was $20,302. Secondary schools, on average, had a higher base salary, depending on the region of the country and the type of community.

The salaries in NAIS schools range from $14,950 to $68,165 in day schools and $16,500 to $51,438 in boarding schools. Among the 10 percent paying the highest salaries, the range is $52,666 to $68,165; among the 50 percent in the middle, $35,000 to $46,095.

More private school teachers than public school teachers receive *in-kind* (nonmonetary) and other benefits. Teachers in boarding schools, for example, may be provided with housing and board, often for their whole family. Many schools offer tuition waivers for faculty children, and some make grants for college tuition. Some also give grants to teachers for graduate study and support their participation in professional associations and societies. Teachers in non-Catholic religious schools and in nonsectarian schools are more likely to receive these kinds of benefits than teachers in Catholic schools.

A few private schools belong to the Teachers Insurance and Annuity Association College Retirement Equities Fund (TIAA–CREF, described in Chapter 6) and to TIAA insurance programs. Other schools provide similar benefits, usually health and hospitalization insurance and retirement. Fringe benefits are so diverse that people interested in private school teaching should inquire about them at each school at which they are considering employment.

FIRSTHAND ACCOUNTS

Lisa Johnson is an elementary school teacher who has worked throughout North Carolina in grades 3 through 5. Since receiving her bachelor's degree from the University of North Carolina at Chapel Hill, she has earned a master's degree in elementary education and become certified by the National Board for Professional Teaching Standards. Currently she is working on a doctorate in hopes of becoming a teacher educator. She describes what her work is like and identifies some upsides and downsides.

Portraying the work of an elementary school teacher is difficult, for each day comprises unique and extraordinary experiences. An elementary school classroom consists of a wide array of students from a variety of backgrounds. We elementary school teachers would like to think that when students enter the school building, they leave the outside world behind and are ready to soak up the knowledge and content we are imparting. However, the reality is just the opposite: Students bring a lot to school. There are students who live in two-parent homes with all the amenities possible who feel an incredible amount of pressure and anxiety to be the smartest, most advanced children in the class. Then there are students who come from homes where they are parents to two younger siblings for whom they must cook and care.

All teachers at my grade level teach the same curriculum. How we present it sets apart instructional leaders from the general population of teachers. I look at my students as opportunities, each with his or her own background and experiences on which I can build. Starting with the students versus starting with the curriculum shows students their importance in their education. Emphasizing the value of diversity, of sharing and discussing differences, allows interaction and promotes accepting behaviors in children as early as kindergarten.

This is easy to say but challenging to implement. My days can be long, and my nights even longer. Being in the classroom from 8:00 A.M. until 3:30 P.M. is only about half of my job. I attend meetings and workshops, communicate daily with parents, complete assessments and student profiles, and collaborate with other teachers at my grade level. I act as a mentor to beginning teachers and a coach to student teachers. I take home papers on which to provide feedback, and I consistently look for new and innovative ways to present information that my students can relate to and apply in their own lives. I must keep abreast of new policies and be an advocate for programs that I deem beneficial to the education of my students. Further, at least two days of the week, I attend graduate classes for my advanced degree.

Upsides and Downsides

As I look back over my career, memories of many moments of absolute joy fill my mind. The pure phenomenon of being able to teach is reward beyond imagination. The opportunity to inspire children through a summer book club, or the spark in a child's eye when the light bulb finally comes on after weeks of work, will hook any person meant to be a teacher.

Being able to work in a field that always is involved in research and innovation is stimulating. I find myself poring over recently published educational journals wondering how I can better teach my children and assist other teachers. I look for ways to educate myself continuously and build my repertoire of strategies and effective practices.

The downside of education is the lack of hours in the day and money in the budget. When you know that a student could master the concept of division if you just spent thirty more minutes with him, or when you cannot attend a workshop on mathematics problem solving because the county has run out of funds for staff development, teaching can be frustrating. Education is not on the priority list of those who control the money, or there would never be a shortage of paper or a child without a book bag or a teacher denied access to continuing education.

Deborah Neely teaches ninth-grade English at Schroder Paideia Academy in Cincinnati, Ohio. She holds a B.A. in sociology from Miami University, in Oxford, Ohio, and an M.Ed. with a specialization in reading from Xavier University in Cincinnati. She describes how she got started and what the work is like.

As an adolescent, I started a small summer daycare program in the backyard of my home. The children came and sat at the picnic table, and I taught them spelling and crafts. Around lunchtime I served them peanut butter and jelly sandwiches, milk, and cookies. That was my first teaching experience.

In college I majored in social work and pursued that career for a short time. In the process I encountered many children with difficult home environments. The majority saw no hopeful future, and the look of despair in their eyes was daunting. I wanted to work with this type of child and thought that I could have more of an effect in the classroom. I returned to college and got certified in English and reading. Soon after, I completed a master's degree as a reading specialist. Today I work in an urban school in Cincinnati, Ohio.

Nothing can fully prepare a teacher for the teaching experience until he or she steps into a classroom and learns firsthand. Little of my college training equipped me with the tenacity I have needed to survive in an urban school. When I began teaching, I had one thought firmly in mind: to have a positive impact. As a ninth-grade English teacher, I find that one of my biggest challenges has been to help students understand the importance of respect and compassion. When those behaviors are absent, education is impeded. In my classroom we talk about what those behaviors mean and why they matter. I reinforce our discussions through my interaction with students and other adults and through literature and writing. It is not always an easy task. I remember a particularly challenging day when I found myself teetering on the edge. A student walked up and said, "Excuse me, Mrs. Neely. I'm finished with my assignment. Can I help Andre edit his paper?" I began to see the value of our class discussions.

Not all of my students have a strong command of the English language, an insatiable desire to read, or a hefty appetite to learn. I continually examine my lessons to find the right fit. I know that each class has its own personality, and I adjust accordingly. I am not always successful, but I never stop trying.

Upsides and Downsides

At times the job is unforgiving and very demanding. Yet the rewards do come: the senior who comes back the next year to tell me how well he is doing in college, the student who stops by my room after school to share a word or two.

A part of teaching that gets downplayed is teachers' responsibilities outside the classroom. In addition to attending staff and parent meetings, teachers serve as committee members, club advisers, team leaders, or coaches. In my school, teachers of English, math, science, social studies, Spanish, and special education work in teams. We handle the academic concerns and the discipline matters of the students we share. Once a week, after school, each teacher offers an hour-long help session for students in need of tutoring. The days are long and draining, but being a team member is rewarding. We bring ideas and concerns to the team for feedback. We plan interdisciplinary projects and activities for our students. We laugh or cry over coffee. Sometimes we disagree, but we have a mutual respect, and we rely on one another.

CHAPTER 3

SCHOOL ADMINISTRATION

In the last half of the twentieth century, as schooling in the United States became more universal and the population doubled, the need for school administration and management grew tremendously. The number and the kinds of school administrators increased, and changes and expansions in school administration occurred for various reasons. As well, there were new expectations that principals assume instructional leadership roles in their schools.

School systems that serve essentially all young people from kindergarten through high school are a recent development. With the country's population exploding from more than 90 million in 1910 to more than 282 million in 2000, and with a much larger percentage of school-age youngsters staying in school than ever before, it goes unrecognized that education is better, curriculum offerings are broader, and management and administration are vastly improved. In 1950, only about 35 percent of the U.S. population twenty-five years of age and older had completed twelve years of school. By 2000 that figure had risen to 87 percent.

The public, business, and government have demanded richer and more varied curriculum offerings to meet the needs of young people for life and occupations in a rapidly changing global society. Such demands require more extensive facilities and resources as well as a consolidation of efforts in educational planning and management. Particularly since World War II, a massive effort to reduce the excessive number of small school districts has created greater management challenges and more administrative positions. Consolidation reduced the number of school districts from 127,531 in 1931 to 14,928 in 2000.

Principals are a keystone of high-achieving elementary and secondary schools. They occupy positions of responsibility and leadership. Increasingly, they are exhorted to build teams, to model the highest professional and ethical standards, to practice efficient and effective management, to exhibit political savvy, to use effective communication skills, and to be instructional leaders. Because of the increase in expectations for these school leaders, state and national policy makers have initiated performance-based expectations for prospective principals and superintendents based on the Interstate School Leaders Licensure Consortium standards, adopted in 1996 and now used throughout the country.

Another leading player in schools is the superintendent, the administrative head of a school district. As might be expected, the greater the responsibility of new and larger school districts, the more powerful and the more political the position of the superintendent. The superintendent is the "point person," the individual on whom both praise and criticism settle. Even though the days of the publicly elected superintendent are gone (in most districts), local boards of education control selection of superintendents and terms of office. In the continuing controversy over the quality and the direction of education, the political vulnerability of today's superintendent has made the longevity of employment extremely tenuous. Terms of office in large cities are particularly short.

The superintendent's supporting cast varies in size. In large systems it may include deputy, associate, and assistant superintendents; principals; and assistant principals. The latter two types of players are building-level leaders, administrative heads and subheads of elementary, middle, junior high, and high schools. Other players include central or regional office administrators and supervisors and curriculum specialists.

This chapter discusses careers as principals and superintendents and their deputies, associates, or assistants. Chapter 4 will address careers as middle-level administrators and supervisors.

PRINCIPALS

There are four levels of principals: elementary, middle, junior high, and high school. However, few preparation programs for principals exist at levels other than elementary and secondary school (which includes junior high and high school). Most state licensure regulations provide only for elementary and secondary school principals.

The basic administrative jobs in a school are management and instructional leadership. Principals (and in larger schools, assistant principals) are charged with leadership, discipline, and management at the building level. National studies and reviews of education have affirmed the importance of dynamic, effective, inspired leadership of the building unit. The result has been greater recognition and more attention to the role of principal.

The principal is a key person in a school. Along with teacher leaders, he or she (an increasing number of principals are women) sets the tone for success. Principals work with, and have administrative responsibility for, teachers, specialists, students, support staff, and nonlicensed employees. They interact with parents, the public, and the community, and they serve as the link between the staff and the students of a school building and the school district's central office.

Chapter 2 pointed out the difficulty of generalizing about the job of the teacher. In the same way, the job of the principal defies generalization. There is no typical principal because principalships vary greatly. The principal's job depends on the enrollment of the school; the nature of the student body; the size of the school district; the district's per-pupil expenditure; the community, regional, and state context; and more.

The principal is a school's chief executive officer. He or she is the leader, the head of the faculty. The name *principal* is most likely rooted in the British term *principal teacher*, referring to a time when all principals taught in addition to managing their school (still the case in some small schools).

Assistant principals' duties are determined by or in consultation with the principal. Student discipline and attendance most often are among those duties.

Principals and assistant principals are appointed to their jobs, usually by the superintendent of schools with the advice and the consent of the school board. In school districts that have moved to site-based management, teachers often have a voice in selection of the principal. Most principals and assistant principals do not have tenure.

Attracting and Keeping Principals

School districts are eager to attract and keep principals. Yet there is a growing shortage of principals. The increasing complexity of the job has placed new demands on administrators. Some potential applicants are concerned that the compensation is insufficient compared with the responsibilities. Others are reluctant to take on the myriad administrative tasks involved in the job. Table 3.1 lists the factors that discourage potential applicants.

As the table indicates, the top-ranked barrier is "compensation insufficient compared to responsibilities," followed by "job too stressful" and "too much time required." These factors are similar for all three levels of schools—elementary, middle/junior high, and senior high—and for urban, suburban, and rural communities.

Yet almost 40 percent of practicing principals responding to a 1998 study of elementary school principals described their morale as "excellent," and an additional 54 percent characterized it as "good but could be better." Slightly more than 50 percent said that they would become principals "if starting out all over again," and an additional 33 percent said that they "probably would." Only 16 percent indicated that they probably or certainly would not make the same choice again.

Most principals are satisfied with their jobs and identify their deep engagement with students and teachers as the major reason for their job satisfaction. Because the job of a principal is stressful, many school dis-

Table 3.1 Issues and Concerns Discouraging Applicants for the Principalship

Issue or Concern	Percentage of Respondents Expressing Concern
Compensation insufficient compared to responsibilities	60
Job too stressful	32
Too much time required	27
Difficult to satisfy parents and/or community	14
Societal problems make it difficult to focus on instruction	13
Few experienced teachers interested	12
Testing and accountability pressures	7
Inadequate funding	3
Would lose tenure as teacher	1
No tenure for position	1

Source: Adapted from *Is There a Shortage of Qualified Candidates for Openings in the Principalship? An Exploratory Study*, by Educational Research Service, 1998, Arlington, VA: Author.

tricts now are exploring or implementing mentoring programs for principals. Principals consistently identify mentoring as the most important support in their initial days as a new principal. However, fewer than 50 percent of schools have a formal mentoring program for new principals.

What Being a Principal Is Like

Describing the length of a principal's typical workweek or the usual duties of a principal is far easier than painting a picture of what being a principal is like. There is hardly a typical day in the life of a principal. There are so many different schools and principalships, and the job has so much diversity. Yet it is possible to generalize about a few aspects of the job.

A principal's day can be full of excitement, pressure, conflict, intensity, pathos, joy, sadness, confusion, and order. To keep on an even keel, principals must know who they are, what they believe, and what the limits and the license of their job are. Whether alone or with one or more assistants, the principal is responsible for the various aspects of managing a school: planning; scheduling; developing programs and curriculum; supervising personnel, student activities, and student behavior; providing instructional leadership; and fostering professional development.

The foregoing duties are responsibilities within the building. Principals also must maintain relationships with parents and citizens in the community and with the school district's central office. Relationships with parents and citizens vary greatly, just as communities and traditions of home-school interaction differ.

In the realm of central office relationships and responsibilities, the principal must deal with budget, personnel evaluation, selection of new staff, attendance, student testing, school board decisions, legislative mandates, legal and court actions, and public relations. Many of the foregoing have ramifications or corresponding responsibilities at the building level, no matter how broad or restricted the services of the school.

Elementary School Principals

There are about 68,000 elementary schools in the United States. All have a principal of some kind, and some have assistant principals. Very small schools have teaching principals or a principal who is responsible for more than one school. The grades typically included in elementary schools are

K–6. Sometimes there is a prekindergarten as well. Different configurations, as well as size, setting, locale, type of student body, and financial support, dictate differences in administrative responsibility. As a consequence, there are many types of elementary school principalships.

The size of an elementary school is a major determinant of the scope and the complexity of the job. Administrative responsibility, a principal's relationships with teachers and students, and the number of duties that are delegated to assistant principals and teachers vary greatly depending on the size of a school.

Three-fourths of the nation's public school principals head elementary schools. Approximately 60 percent of these principals hold a master's degree, 27 percent an educational specialist license, and 9 percent a doctoral degree. Only about 3 percent do not have a graduate degree or an advanced license. The average elementary school principal had at least eleven years of teaching experience before becoming a principal.

The principal's contract may be for ten to twelve months of work. Increasingly, principals are on eleven- or twelve-month contracts because of the complexity and scope of their responsibilities. In 2001 the average annual salary for elementary school principals was $73,114. However, the range in salaries was great. Salaries are reviewed later in this chapter.

Middle and Junior High School Principals

The middle school and the junior high school have been labeled *middle-level schools*. The grades in middle-level schools are typically in one of three configurations: 6–8, 6–9, or 7–8. The middle school often is designed to serve students who are preadolescents and early adolescents. The physiological, glandular, intellectual, moral, and social-emotional changes experienced during early adolescence constitute the most substantial shift a human being undergoes. Distinguished psychologist David Elkind points out that the growth of more complex thought systems raises the early adolescent to new heights of mental operations, yet lowers him or her to new depths. What Elkind means is that the early adolescent becomes excessively egocentric in thought. Accordingly the middle school student may begin to perceive himself or herself as the center of the universe. The dynamic changes in students during the middle school years explain why middle-level principals (and middle school teachers) have fascinating yet uniquely challenging jobs. They must have a deep understanding of early adolescence. Anyone who has worked in a middle-level school knows that this age group can be among the most exciting to work with—and among the most difficult, as well.

The middle-level school also is an institution of transition. In the elementary school, usually one teacher teaches a given class for the entire day. In the middle-level school, departmentalization (a different teacher for each subject, students moving from classroom to classroom) begins either gradually or abruptly, depending on how the school is organized. Increasingly, middle-level schools are designed to support teacher teams that work with a cohort of students. Team planning for instruction in the core subjects occurs, and students have greater opportunity to form friendships with peers. The principal must orient students and their parents to the new organization. More responsibility is put on the student. How to help the student accept it is the worry of every middle-level school principal.

Middle-level school principals report working more than fifty hours per week. The workload includes managing the school, administering personnel, addressing student behavior problems, developing programs, supervising teachers, evaluating teachers, supervising student activities, communicating with the district office, maintaining parent and community relations, and planning and implementing professional development. Very few middle-level school principals teach.

More information on the middle-level school principalship is available from publications by the National Middle School Association, the National Association of Elementary School Principals, the National Association of Secondary School Principals, and publications listed in the Bibliography.

High School Principals

About 74 percent of high school principals administer three- or four-year high schools, grades 9–12 or 10–12. The four-year unit is the most common. The size of the schools varies greatly. Typically, urban and suburban high schools are large. For example, in a populous state like Florida, the number of students in a public high school can be more than 2,500, whereas in a rural state like Alaska, the average number of students in a public high school is 491. The national average in public secondary schools is 706.

The high school principal administers an institution with unique functions and problems. Some students are college bound, others terminate their formal education with graduation, and still others drop out before completing school. In general, high school principals spend their time in a variety of ways to provide all students with the best education that the school can offer. High school principals indicate a number of types of responsibilities in a typical workweek, including the following:

- Management (calendar, office, budget, memos)
- Personnel (evaluating, advising, conferring, recruiting)
- Student activities (meetings, supervision, planning)
- Program development (curriculum, instructional leadership)
- Student behavior (discipline, attendance, meetings)
- District office (meetings, task forces, reports)
- Community (PTA, advisory groups, parent conferences)
- Planning (annual, long-range)
- Professional development (reading, conferences)

When queried about the major obstacles they face, high school principals identified five factors:

1. Time taken by administrative detail
2. Lack of time
3. Variation in ability of teachers
4. Inability to obtain funding
5. Apathetic or irresponsible parents

Other concerns voiced by principals included insufficient space and physical facilities, problem students, staff resistance to change, and poor communication.

Preparation for Becoming a Principal

Most states now specify a master's degree in educational administration and prior teaching experience as prerequisites for becoming a principal. Table 3.2 lists the areas of study frequently required of prospective principals by university educational administration programs. These courses often are aligned with the Interstate School Leaders Licensure Consortium standards for educational leaders.

People who aspire to administrative leadership in schools are well advised to think about more than the educational background that they need to qualify for a position. In the early stages of considering a career as principal, it is best to assess why one wants to become a principal and what one's aptitude is for the job. Teachers have a unique vantage point from which to observe the job. They are on the inside of the school, and they can view the principal in all kinds of situations. (They never see the whole picture or feel the full responsibility, though.)

There are at least four ways in which a person might learn about the preparation needed to be a principal. They are not mutually exclusive.

1. Consult university catalogs and review the requirements to complete a program in educational administration with either an elementary, middle, junior high, or high school emphasis.
2. Review the areas of study and the courses that principals have found most useful on the job (for example, as reported by many principals in surveys or by individual principals in interviews).

Table 3.2 University Requirements for Educational Administration

Study Required by Most Universities	Study Required by Some Universities
Administrative theory	Counseling and guidance
Community relations	Ethics and decision making
Curriculum theory	Foundations in research and assessment
Effective communication	Internships
Historical foundations of education	Introduction to inquiry
Instructional leadership	Perspectives on diversity in education
Personnel administration	Perspectives on the adult learner
Principles and practices of instructional supervision	Politics of education
	Psychology of learning
School finance and budgeting	Systems theory
School law	Tests and measurements

Source: Adapted from a list produced by the National Association of Secondary School Principals and the National Association of Elementary School Principals, Reston, VA.

3. Inquire at a state department of education about licensure requirements.
4. Consider reasons for becoming a principal, explore the kind of principal one wants to be, and then decide how to prepare to be that kind of principal, within legal and academic requirements.

Preparation for a principalship requires graduate study. Virtually all practicing principals have at least a master's degree, and a high percentage have graduate work beyond that credential. All states require a person to have a license in school administration to be employed as a principal at any level.

Most principals were teachers before they started graduate study. For a prospective principal, graduate study often parallels work as a teacher. Taking courses in the evening, on Saturday, and during the summer makes graduate study affordable. Because of the shortage of principals, some states provide stipends and grants-in-aid for teachers interested in becoming principals. As well, some school systems provide institutes for teachers who would like to explore their own leadership potential.

Many universities now require an internship as part of graduate study in administration. This often is a yearlong internship in a school. The prospective principal must dedicate time and effort in concentrated work-study on the firing line under the supervision of an experienced principal and a university professor. The internship gives prospective principals and their supervisors an opportunity to examine potential and to test ability and aptitude in a real situation. Most principals who have served internships rate them as highly useful or essential.

Career Patterns of Principals

Nearly all principals have been teachers. Experience in the classroom is considered by most educators to be essential for that career. The National Association of Elementary School Principals, the National Association of Secondary School Principals, and the American Association of School Administrators officially endorse successful classroom schoolteaching as a requirement for a principalship. Why? Most educational leaders recognize that principals are instructional leaders, and being a leader in instruction means understanding what teaching involves and having successful experience in that role. A small number of educators and political leaders contend that a good manager, irrespective of background, would qualify as a school administrator. This viewpoint is illustrated in Chicago, New York, and Washington, D.C., where managers have been hired to bring solutions to the problems of inner-city schools. However, others raise concerns that such a manager does not have the needed background in teaching and student learning that is at the very core of the educational enterprise. Most states require principals to have teaching experience and advanced study, usually a master's degree in educational administration. There is a hierarchy and a career ladder for those who choose educational leadership as a career.

Finding Employment as a Principal

Principals find employment in much the same way that teachers do. Beginners register with a placement office at a university where they hope to complete advanced preparation, either a master's degree or other appropriate graduate training, and they solicit recommendations from professors and other educators who know their work. When a prospective principal has completed an internship as a part of graduate training, the recommendations of the cooperating principal and the university supervisor can be telling. For experienced principals, there is an informal network through which information and recommendations pass by word of mouth. A wise candidate will keep all alternatives operating.

The track record of a prospective principal in a teaching role or an assistant principalship, if it is solid and strong, is an asset. In fact, many prospective principals begin graduate study in administration on the encouragement of principals or superintendents for whom they have worked.

The assistant principal position is often a stepping-stone to a principalship, particularly at the middle and high school levels. Many high school principals were assistant principals in high schools before taking the top building-level job. A substantial percentage were assistant principals or principals in elementary or middle-level schools before becoming a high school principal. High school principals most frequently attribute their first appointment as principal to success as an assistant principal and to a successful job interview.

Salary and Fringe Benefits

Like almost everything else about principals' jobs, salaries defy generalization. Averages miss all the distinctions caused by size of school, wealth of school district, years of experience, and level of education. Several ways of presenting salary figures help tell the story. Table 3.3 presents principals' and assistant principals' salaries in 2001–02 by student enrollment in the district.

The hierarchy in school administration is apparent in the salaries paid principals in elementary schools compared with those paid principals in high schools. However, an elementary school principal can earn more than a junior or senior high school principal. The factor of size makes a difference. For example, the average salary of an elementary school principal in a school district with 25,000 students or more is $75,301, while the average salary of a high school principal in a school district with 300 to 2,499 students is $71,123.

Per-pupil expenditure in a district—that is, the amount a district spends per student on education—is another factor in the size of salaries. The

Table 3.3 Mean of Average Salaries Paid to Principals and Assistant Principals (in Dollars), by School District Enrollment, 2001–02

	Systems of 25,000 or More Students	Systems of 10,000–24,999 Students	Systems of 2,500–9,999 Students	Systems of 300–2,499 Students
Principals				
Elementary school	75,301	74,563	75,585	66,219
Junior high/middle school	79,873	79,716	80,624	69,066
Senior high school	87,744	87,986	87,313	71,123
Assistant Principals				
Elementary school	59,840	60,510	62,698	56,930
Junior high/middle school	62,523	64,343	66,396	59,927
Senior high school	67,096	68,915	70,218	60,549

Source: From *Mean of Average, Lowest, and Highest Salaries Paid to Personnel in Selected Professional Positions in Reporting School Systems, by Enrollment Group, Per Pupil Expenditures, and Geographic Region* (2001–02 ed.), by Educational Research Service, 2002, Arlington, VA: Author.

wealth of a district typically determines the salary paid school personnel, including principals. (Wealth almost always is directly related to the socioeconomic level of residents and the tax base of properties.) District wealth is so important a factor that a smaller school in a wealthier district often will pay its principal more than a larger school in a poorer district. Table 3.4 reports salaries of principals and assistant principals in 2001–02 by per-pupil expenditure.

As Table 3.4 indicates, there is a trend toward larger salaries for principals and assistant principals in school districts with larger per-pupil expenditures. For example, a middle school principal in a school district with per-pupil expenditures of $9,000 or more has a mean salary of $85,922, while a middle school principal in a school district with per-pupil expenditures of less than $6,000 has a mean salary of $70,847.

Salaries also vary by state, and this variation is related to per-pupil expenditure and district and state wealth. It usually is a function of cost of living. Additional information on salary includes salary ranges for states and regions. The Educational Research Service in Arlington, Virginia, con-

Table 3.4 Mean of Mean Salaries Paid to Principals and Assistant Principals (in Dollars), by Per-Pupil Expenditure, 2001–02

	Per-Pupil Expenditure					
	$9,000 or More	$8,000–$8,999	$7,000–$7,999	$6,000–$6,999	Less than $6,000	All Systems
Principals						
Elementary school	80,235	73,048	72,635	72,686	66,457	73,114
Junior high/middle school	85,922	79,016	77,704	77,161	70,847	78,176
Senior high school	91,088	81,692	83,507	82,691	72,428	83,944
Assistant Principals						
Elementary school	69,492	63,784	60,407	59,834	54,951	60,672
Junior high/middle school	72,869	67,288	63,988	62,518	57,699	64,375
Senior high school	76,127	70,000	67,619	66,011	60,091	67,822

Source: From *Mean of Average, Lowest, and Highest Salaries Paid to Personnel in Selected Professional Positions in Reporting School Systems, by Enrollment Group, Per Pupil Expenditure Level, and Geographic Region, 2001–2002,* by Educational Research Service, 2002, Arlington, VA: Author.

ducts periodic studies on salary range. Recent data from an exploratory study of principals suggest that almost 60 percent of respondents thought the compensation was insufficient compared with the responsibilities.

Support for Beginning Principals

Many principals mention mentoring by good and experienced principals as the most important kind of support needed in the initial months as a new principal. Unfortunately, such support is not common. However, in a 1998 exploratory survey by the Educational Research Service, just under half of the superintendents interviewed indicated that their districts had a formal induction or mentoring program for new principals. Table 3.5 reports the results by type of district. As the table indicates, 45 percent of rural school districts had some type of formal mentoring program for new principals, 48 percent of suburban school districts, and 54 percent of urban school districts. In the study, both superintendents who had support programs and those who did not thought that such assistance was critical to the success of new principals. These support programs are increasingly aimed at instructional leadership skills, with a focus on teaching and learning.

Support for Professional Development and Graduate Study

Tuition reimbursement for graduate study, like so many other benefits, varies by size and wealth of district. Principals and superintendents may want to ascertain whether their school district reimburses them for tuition for professional development and graduate study.

Insurance Benefits

Insurance benefits for administrators and supervisors (except superintendents) are grouped together because they are usually the same. They are at least comparable to, and normally better than, those provided for teachers. Benefits and the percentage of districts providing them appear in Table 3.5. The percentage of districts that pay the full cost of a particular benefit also is noted.

Not reported is the percentage of districts offering family coverage for each of the health benefits. It, too, varies by the district's per-pupil expenditure. Married candidates for an administrative position should ask about coverage for dependents.

Table 3.5 Insurance Benefits Provided for Administrators and Supervisors by School Districts

Type	Districts Providing (%)	Districts Fully Paying Premiums (%)
Hospitalization coverage	97.1	85.0
Medical/surgical coverage	95.8	84.9
Major medical coverage	96.2	85.3
Physical examination	32.0	26.3
Dental care coverage	81.4	86.6
Vision care coverage	50.0	82.7
Prescription drugs coverage	85.3	84.4
Group life insurance	77.5	76.9
Accidental death and dismemberment	44.4	ND
Professional liability insurance	67.2	ND

ND = No data

These are the most recent data available. In a telephone conversation in January 2003, an Educational Research Service manager said that the organization has not conducted a more recent study of these benefits because they tend not to change rapidly.

Source: Adapted from *Fringe Benefits for Administrators and Supervisors in Public Schools, 1994–95*, by Educational Research Service, 1995, Arlington, VA: Author.

About 78 percent of districts report providing group life insurance for administrators and supervisors. The range of policy amounts is $2,000 to $500,000, depending on factors such as salary, the availability of options to increase the value of the policy, and enrollment in the school district. For individuals, the mean face value of the group life insurance policy is $65,401.

Insurance and fringe benefits for administrators and supervisors have improved over the last two decades.

Retirement Programs

All administrators and supervisors participate in a retirement system of some kind. Typically, districts support defined-benefit pension plans through a state teachers retirement system. Such plans represent a significant fringe benefit for educators. Corporations are severely curtailing traditional defined-benefit pension plans in favor of 401(k)s, which are largely dependent on employees' savings.

In almost all retirement systems, both the employee (the administrator or the supervisor) and the school district contribute. The percentage of contribution varies by state and school district, as does the period necessary for *vesting* (that is, for the employer's contribution to become the property of the employee). Some retirement systems require a substantial contribution by the employer; others prescribe that employer and employee pay an equal share.

Another kind of retirement income is Social Security. Because public education personnel are government employees of sorts, some states have not made administrators, supervisors, or other school personnel eligible for Social Security.

A third type of retirement income is 403(b)s and IRAs. Created by Congress in the late 1970s and early 1980s, these voluntary, tax-deferred savings plans are available in all school systems. They set maximum contributions that educators can invest through a payroll plan. They are an attractive supplemental retirement option.

Severance Pay

Because administrators usually do not have tenure, terminations may be abrupt. As a consequence, severance pay (usually in a lump sum) is more important for them than for teachers. Severance pay can be helpful in a number of instances: when an administrator or a supervisor resigns, when a superintendent leaves and the school board wants a new administrative team, when a board wants to encourage early retirement, or when regular retirement comes. Other factors influencing payments to departing administrators are years of service, age at severance, early retirement incentives, and retirement provisions.

Leave Provisions

Leave policies are determined by local school systems. Vacation leave is usually provided for administrators who have a twelve-month contract. For other types of leave, there is considerable variation both in the extent of coverage and in the percentage of districts granting them, according to the Educational Research Service's figures.

Critical fringe benefits—that is, health insurance and retirement—are not transferable from one state to another. Some states have buy-in provisions for work experience in another state if official documentation of experience is presented, but the number of years a person can purchase is usually limited. Before signing a contract, administrators or supervisors taking new employment in another state should check the effective beginning date of health insurance and the years that can be credited toward retirement. Fringe benefits often are easier to negotiate before signing a contract than afterward.

SUPERINTENDENTS

The top-level positions in school administration are those of superintendent of schools and the superintendent's deputies, associates, and assistants. The job of chief administrative officer of a school system has become particularly difficult and vulnerable in recent years. The rapidly changing world, new expectations of schools, different lifestyles, changes in social and moral values, desegregation, drugs and violence in schools, increases in the variety of ethnic populations, shifts in funding patterns, declining resources, an aging teaching force, and demands for accountability are among the problems that make difficult times, and often short tenure, for top-level school administrators. When situations become strained and conflict in decision making creates turmoil, the top person is the first to be replaced. Superintendents usually work on term contracts and do not have tenure. They are the easiest to fire. Their average tenure, according to the National School Boards Association's 2002 Council of Urban Boards of Education Survey, is five years, although the media often report it as two-and-a-half years. Longer tenure for superintendents has an impact on the success of school districts. High turnover undermines reform efforts.

One way to explore the prospects of becoming a superintendent is to examine the kinds of people who now hold the position, their routes to the job, and the nature of the job. Such inquiry is not easy because there also is great diversity among superintendents and wide variety in their circumstances. Geographic location, size of school district, diversity of the district's population, and level of support provided to the school district are major dimensions of difference. However, keeping those variables in mind, it is possible to sketch the superintendency in broad strokes and report some specifics about the job.

What Being a Superintendent Is Like

The characteristic that most clearly distinguishes types of superintendents is the size of the school district. Why? Larger school districts are more complex organizations, and the demands placed on superintendents are considerable.

The U.S. Department of Education's National Center for Education Statistics reports the number of school districts and the corresponding percentage of students in each of eight enrollment categories. Table 3.6 presents the data. As the table indicates, 3,921 of the nation's 14,505 school districts enroll 81.8 percent of the nation's students. At the extreme of schools enrolling 10,000 students or more, 817 of the nation's school districts (5.6 percent) account for 50.8 percent of its students. At the extreme of schools enrolling fewer than 1,000 students, 7,193 (49.6 percent) of the

Table 3.6 Number of Public School Districts and Percentage of Students Enrolled, by Size of District, 1999–2000

Enrollment Size of District	Number of School Districts	Percentage of Students Enrolled
25,000 or more	238	32.1
10,000–24,999	579	18.7
5,000–9,999	1,036	15.4
2,500–4,999	2,068	15.6
1,000–2,499	3,457	12.1
600–999	1,814	3.1
300–599	2,081	2.0
1–299	3,298	1.0
Size not reported	357	—
Total	14,505	

Source: From *Digest of Education Statistics*, by National Center for Education Statistics, 2001, Washington, DC: Author.

nation's school districts account for 6.1 percent of the students. Clearly, there are many small school districts in the country, in places where the population is sparse.

Populations are concentrated in cities, so people often assume that cities have large school districts. That is true, but some county districts are larger than city districts.

Because of these great variations in enrollment size of districts, there is no typical or average school superintendent. A superintendency in a school district with a small enrollment may well be no more complicated than the principalship of a school in a large district.

The superintendent is responsible for all aspects of a school district's operation. He or she either handles directly or delegates the various tasks and duties outlined in Chapter 4:

- Planning
- Development
- Operation
- Evaluation
- Curriculum and instruction
- Special education
- Guidance and psychological services
- Personnel
- Library and media
- Materials and supplies
- Plant maintenance
- Business affairs
- Food services
- Transportation
- Communications
- Community relations
- State and federal programs

In a few very small school districts in rural America, the superintendent is the lone top officer and manages all those responsibilities (some are not even required in very small districts). When many of the tasks are delegated, the superintendent spends much of his or her time exercising leadership, coordinating the activities of staff, planning and assessing future needs, selecting highly competent people for key administrative positions, supporting those people, and maintaining relationships with state offices of education, the school board, and the community.

Preparation for Becoming a Superintendent

Preparation for the superintendency is very much like preparation for other school administration positions. The superintendent may in fact have completed all his or her formal training before becoming a superintendent, either during a principalship or in the position of assistant superintendent.

Patterns of preparation vary as much as the superintendency itself. Most superintendents have earned at least a master's degree. One complaint about graduate preparation is the lack of full-time study. However, much of the preparation for such a position consists of on-the-job training and learning from experience. The fact that many superintendents in large school districts got their experience in large districts demonstrates that much is learned on the job.

Career Patterns of Superintendents

Almost all superintendents of schools in the United States today began their careers as teachers and then became principals. There followed a series of steps in the hierarchy of central administration, from small systems to larger ones and from central office staff member to assistant superintendent and then to superintendent.

Most superintendents are appointed. They serve at the pleasure of their local school board on a contract or a letter of appointment, often with a specified term of office.

Finding Employment as a Superintendent

Employing superintendents is usually much more complicated than hiring administrators at lower levels, particularly in larger school districts. Openings are publicized widely. Candidates sometimes apply on the basis of public advertisements or information from placement offices. More frequently they learn about an opening through the superintendents' collegial network to which they belong. Not infrequently, candidates are sought out by a school board itself or by a consultant hired by a board. In any case the school board establishes goals, criteria, procedures, and a timeline for selecting a superintendent.

Gaining a superintendency may in part involve being at the right place at the right time. On the other hand, an appointment from inside the school district is probably based more on a school board's observation of the candidate's performance over time.

Salary and Fringe Benefits

Salaries for superintendents are idiosyncratic. Some generalizations can be made. For example, large districts usually pay more than small districts, and wealthy districts more than poor districts. However, there are numerous exceptions and caveats.

Table 3.7 presents one way to explore salaries. The 2001–02 contract salary of all superintendents reporting in an Educational Research Service study averaged $121,794. The average salary for superintendents in 1995 was $94,229. Thus there has been an average increase of $27,565, which represents a 5.8 percent increase each year since 1995. Superintendents in school districts with 25,000 students or more have an average salary of $163,737, whereas those in school districts with 300 to 2,499 students have an average salary of $96,999. Additional factors that influence superin-

Table 3.7 Mean of Mean Salaries Paid to Superintendents, Deputy or Associate Superintendents, and Assistant Superintendents (in Dollars), by School District Enrollment, 2001–02

	Systems of 25,000 or More Students	Systems of 10,000–24,999 Students	Systems of 2,500–9,999 Students	Systems of 300–2,499 Students
Superintendent	163,737	132,393	117,251	96,999
Deputy/associate superintendent	115,473	106,272	102,697	76,410
Assistant superintendent	102,424	98,969	94,910	82,935

Source: From *Mean of Average, Lowest, and Highest Salaries Paid to Personnel in Selected Professional Positions in Reporting School Systems, by Enrollment Group, Per Pupil Expenditure, and Geographic Region, 2001–2002,* by Educational Research Service, 2002, Arlington, VA: Author.

tendents' salaries are cost of living in an area, the degree of discretion with budget, support systems, and fringe benefits.

For the top administrative officer, more clearly than for any other administrator in the school district, rewards include certain intangibles that are valuable and satisfying as a part of doing a job—for example, the authority (the legitimate right to exercise power) that goes with the superintendency.

Fringe benefits for superintendents have improved over the last two decades. They are a significant part of income, and many of them are not taxable. Candidates for superintendencies should examine the provisions carefully. Additional benefits not discussed in this section include transportation (some districts provide cars); expense accounts; paid expenses to conventions; civic, social, and/or health club dues; tuition reimbursements; and dues for association membership.

Insurance Benefits

Health and life insurance benefits for superintendents are much the same as those for principals and central office administrators and supervisors, except that they include more provisions and are better.

Retirement Programs

Nearly all districts cover their superintendents through a state retirement system. In almost all retirement systems, both the employee and the school district contribute. The percentage of contribution varies by state and school district, as does the period necessary for vesting. Some retirement systems require a substantial contribution by the employer; others prescribe that employer and employee pay equal shares. Within a state a superintendent can change positions without losing continuity in his or her retirement plan.

Severance Pay

Most superintendents serve under a contract, usually for a specified term—most often three years or more. Therefore severance pay is important, particularly when terminations may be abrupt. As noted earlier, the mean tenure for superintendents is five years. Consequently, candidates for a superintendency must understand the severance package. Policies for paying a departing superintendent a sum of money on leaving tend to differ.

Most districts pay the monetary equivalent of all or some of unused leave days earned. Other factors that influence lump-sum payments are years of service, age at severance, early retirement incentives, and retirement provisions.

Interstate Transfer of Health and Retirement Benefits

Critical fringe benefits such as health insurance and retirement are not transferable from one state to another. Some states have buy-in provisions for work experience in another state if official documentation of experience is presented. But the number of years a person can purchase is limited. Before signing a contract, superintendents taking new employment in another state should check the effective beginning date of health insurance and the years that can be credited toward retirement. As noted elsewhere, fringe benefits often are easier to negotiate before signing a contract than afterward.

FIRSTHAND ACCOUNT

Jim Palermo is the principal of Lufkin Road Middle School in Apex, North Carolina. He holds a B.A. in English, an M.Ed. in counseling, and a Principal's Certificate from North Carolina State University, where he is pursuing an Ed.D. in educational leadership. He discusses what the work is like, describes some upsides and downsides, and offers advice.

> Being a principal means being many things to many people every day. In a school with 1,000 students and 80 certified staff members, the principal is the CEO of a midsized organization and must manage personnel, finances, facilities, and customer relations, as well as supervise teaching and learning—our mission. Fortunately, I have two assistant principals to help share the duties, and I have deliberately defined my role to be the instructional leader, working with staff development, initially licensed teachers, and probationary staff. I also believe that I have an obligation to be a mentor to my assistants so that they will be ready for the principalship. To feel effective, I put in long days, often fifty to sixty hours a week, and work at home evenings and weekends. At least part of every day, I "manage by walk-

ing around" school, in and out of classrooms, talking with students and staff.

Upsides and Downsides

Being a principal is never dull. Every day is different and brings new challenges and opportunities to grow and stretch as a leader and professional educator. The downside is that despite hard work and best efforts, someone is always unhappy and critical. The rewards come from contact with children and staff. At my school I can become disheartened when parents seem to have unrealistic expectations for our performance. When that happens I get out of my office and spend time with the kids.

Advice

The principal today must be an effective manager, but also an instructional leader. You must have at least passing knowledge of the curriculum, a firm grounding in best instructional practices, and an understanding of helping and mentoring models. I believe that the "principal teacher" should have classroom experience prior to administration. You should also be physically fit and know how to manage stress. You should be well grounded in principle and know how to achieve balance in your personal and spiritual life when school threatens to consume you. You should be a lifelong learner and dedicated public servant. You should be humble and a good listener—you derive your leadership from those you lead.

4

CENTRAL OFFICE ADMINISTRATION AND SUPERVISION

Supervisors and middle-level administrators are found in large school districts, where the job of the superintendent of schools is sufficiently complex to require that responsibilities be delegated and where one person cannot oversee and provide leadership and support to all personnel and programs. Of the 100 largest districts in the United States, 98 percent report complex central office administrative structures that include administrators and program supervisors. As might be expected, the 100 largest districts tend to be in cities and counties with large populations. Twenty of the 98 largest districts that report staff by type had 1 percent or more of their staff assigned to district administration—quite a leap from the one-room schoolhouse.

Increasingly these staff serve as instructional leaders who can positively influence schools and communities. A 1999 study published by the U.S. Department of Education found that high-performing schools in high-poverty urban areas had strong instructional leaders who communicated a collective sense of responsibility and spent more time helping teachers attend to instructional issues, as compared with schools where principals focused primarily on administrative matters. Expectations that central office administrators and supervisors offer instructional leadership and supervision arose in the early 1960s, originating in *The Education of American Teachers*, a report by James Conant. It called for reform and revitalization of schools and teacher education.

WHAT BEING A CENTRAL OFFICE ADMINISTRATOR OR SUPERVISOR IS LIKE

The professional personnel who staff a central office ensure that a school district's instructional and curricular programs are effective, have continuity and coherence, and are efficiently administered. They assist in and monitor planning, development, operation, finance, and evaluation of all the areas that are part of running the school system. The traditional areas that they oversee are curriculum, special education, guidance and psychological services, personnel, library and media, materials and supplies, and plant maintenance.

Those who engage in central office administration and supervision have unique perspectives because they interact with many different groups of teachers and administrators. Supervisors, in particular, move back and forth across the different institutional levels and thus gain a larger sense of the schooling enterprise. As educational researcher Michael Fullan points out, these professionals often are able to see how community contexts, fragmentation or coherence of reform initiatives, and changes in the teaching profession can foster or hinder meaningful educational change.

However, as more school systems adopt site-based decision making and management, the number of central office supervisors and program directors may decrease. Site-based management is an approach in which more authority and more discretion over the allocation of resources is transferred to local schools. Thus, author and researcher Malcolm Skilbeck argues, responsibilities that now are largely assumed by supervisors may one day be assumed by teachers as they engage in new roles, like mentoring beginning teachers, coaching colleagues, running staff development programs, coordinating review and adoption of new textbooks, and initiating recruitment and selection of new faculty for their school. Where decision making has been delegated to those closer to students, the role of many central office personnel, particularly instructional and curriculum support staff, has changed from managing to coordinating and advising. However, in management and fiscal matters—for example, in accounting for attendance and school expenditures—a central office responsibility will remain.

Various support services also are managed from the central office: business affairs, food services, transportation, and communications and community relations. In recent years several new areas have been added to the responsibilities of central office staff, among them labor relations, state and federal programs, legislation, legal and judicial oversight, technological developments, and energy coordination. Whether each of these areas is assigned to one individual, or one person carries the responsibility for several, depends on the expertise required and the size of the district. Additionally, as researchers Sharon N. Oja and Alan J. Reiman note in a 1998 synthesis of research on supervision, personal and professional development are becoming more important and more prominent responsibilities in central office programs. Often these are a part of curriculum and instruction, staff development, or induction programs for new educators.

Most middle-level administrators and supervisors are housed with the superintendent at a central location, often in the board of education building. Very large districts have regional centers. Supervisors have offices at these headquarters, but many spend considerable time in the schools helping personnel.

In addition, many central office personnel, particularly in subject areas and general curriculum, plan and facilitate inservice education for teachers and administrators. This role becomes especially important when the school district introduces new content, program innovations, or different organizational structures. For example, many school districts have recently sponsored instruction and workshops on computer literacy, sex education, AIDS prevention, drug and alcohol abuse, school violence, career ladders, and textbook evaluation.

Central office jobs are not always clearly defined by title. A position under a particular title in one district may entail quite different duties from those included in a position by the same title in another district. For example, depending on the district, a guidance person may be a supervisor of psychological counseling, of career counseling, of standardized testing, or of attendance. Discovering the duties of a central office position often is puzzling to prospective applicants.

A person interested in a vacated position may think that the best way to get candid, firsthand information is to talk with the person who left the job. That is perhaps true, but other or new information is often available from official sources. The administration, for example, may be taking the occasion of a change in staff to modify the duties associated with the position, or it may be shifting the position to another department to make central office administration more efficient. The best source of information about the particulars of a position is the job description produced by the personnel office, which is made available when an opening is advertised.

Another source of insight is a district's organization chart. The grouping of areas and the arrangement of the lines of authority tell a lot about the power structure and the program emphasis of the central office. A chart may require some reading between the lines, but it does offer a perspective on how people function operationally.

A prospective applicant for a central office position also should explore the conditions of work, or the work climate. Job descriptions and organization charts will not be of much help in this regard. Instead, the person will have to rely mainly on his or her powers of observation during a visit to the office for an interview.

Redefinition and expansion of middle-management and supervisory positions occur frequently. For example, general administrators may be moved to management of state and federal programs, librarians may become library media specialists, math and science supervisors may extend their responsibility to include computer science, and guidance personnel may take charge of drug and alcohol abuse prevention programs. There are a variety of reasons for such shifts in role and responsibility. People may begin in one job and demonstrate a talent, an interest, or a competence that causes them to be drafted into or attracted to a new role. The administration may discover a new problem or area needing attention. Outside influences may suggest or mandate new procedures or regulations.

Central office professional personnel are in either *line* or *staff* positions. The distinction is important. Line positions are usually management jobs dealing with the elements of school systems that support and make possible the instructional program—for example, compliance with school board, state, and federal regulations and mandates; personnel decisions; payroll; supplies; transportation; and food services. Staff positions are leadership roles in instruction that have a teaching flavor; the duties are neither as precise nor as controlling as those of line personnel. The functions of personnel in staff positions are to consult and advise on personnel matters, curriculum, teaching, materials, media, and resources. In other words, staff people generally serve as guides and supporters, whereas line personnel have administrative authority and responsibility.

Some staff personnel do, of course, have line responsibilities. For example, when departments become large, as happens when two or more school districts are consolidated or when a district adds new staff because of growth in enrollment, the chief of a staff group becomes an administrator (sometimes systemwide). An example is the consolidation of guidance, counseling, testing, and other psychological services into pupil personnel services. Someone from among the staff must administer the specialty area, even though it is largely composed of nonadministrative types.

PREPARATION FOR A CENTRAL OFFICE POSITION

General administrators and supervisors often come from the ranks of administrators at the building level; their jobs are considered promotions in the administrative hierarchy. Their preparation involves an established sequence of graduate study, and many specialize in the area of their work assignment, often with school district support. The combination of study and experience makes possible a progression up the steps of a standard system.

Some line areas, such as transportation, food service, and building and grounds, are too new for formal college preparation programs to have developed, or they have evolved into something different from earlier definitions. People who hold administrative positions in such line areas have relied on experience and frequent short-study programs to make their way up the ladder. The system is dynamic. It makes possible the development of new specialties as new requirements become apparent.

Employees, irrespective of formal training, have a chance to grow and develop and be promoted. People without college degrees may no longer find employment in some of these specialties, but new areas will continue to evolve. In a sense there always will be people who pioneer, who create (or live with the development of) their own specialty.

Specialists in subject areas, guidance, and social and psychological services, who are hired to perform tasks that require advanced training in particular disciplines or areas of knowledge, may come to a central office position from a building assignment or from graduate school. Specialist positions related to teaching, such as social workers, school psychologists, and audiologists, may not require prior teaching experience or licensure as a teacher. These specialists assist in teaching, consult with teachers, and provide valuable counsel to teachers, parents, and administrators. Other specialists need a comprehensive knowledge of teaching, in both content and procedures. They are usually required to have teaching experience and a license to teach, as well as advanced study and degrees in their specialty. Although there are arguments about whether all central office specialists should have teaching experience, most who occupy such positions today have taught before moving to district headquarters.

Almost all central office professional personnel are required to have advanced graduate study and degrees. In fact, most specialist positions, even those at the entry level, require preparation at the graduate level—for example, curriculum and teaching, guidance and counseling, school psychology, and school administration. Some exceptions, most of them not connected with instruction, include business managers; directors of communications, transportation, food service, and building and grounds; energy coordinators; state and federal program officers; and visiting teachers. Personnel in these positions often begin with less than a graduate degree, but increasingly, advanced study is being required. Subject matter specialists begin specialization at the undergraduate level; however, to qualify for a supervisory position, they must have at least a master's degree.

The literature on central office staff is sparse. The reason lies in the difficulty of generalizing about such a widely diverse category of personnel. Even though many specialists work together in school districts, their professional allegiance tends to be to their individual specialty. In addition, no single organization has interest in, or data on, the general category called central office personnel, and central office personnel themselves do not all belong to the same organization. Instead, they belong to professional groups associated with their specialty—the American Association of School Administrators, the American Association of School Personnel Administrators, the American Counseling Association, and the American Library Association, to name a few. More information about central office specialties of interest can be secured by writing to the appropriate organizations. Often, special interest groups (SIGs) have formed within such organizations to convene members whose jobs are alike in order to address their unique interests. Committees in many organizations deliberate on the preparation required for the positions they hold (not infrequently raising standards above those that members have met) and issue standards for entry into their field. Some organizations maintain a list of job openings in their field, but most do not have a full placement service. All publish such materials as journals, newsletters, monographs, and books; some produce films and videotapes; and many have websites. Print and audiovisual media are designed to help members stay current with developments in their field and to use in training programs. All organizations respond promptly and helpfully to requests for materials on organizational purpose and services. Informational flyers and brochures are provided free of charge.

In summary, the contribution of central office administrators and supervisors is well recognized as an important dimension of education and schooling. Such people need insight and skill in helping teachers in their activities with children and adolescents. Yet, as noted earlier, these people represent a wide spectrum of professional backgrounds and expertise. What is common is a growing emphasis on supporting student learning and teacher development. These dual foci support assistance to teachers with both teaching and curriculum development. A fundamental premise of developmental approaches to supervision is that education is a process of growth rather than a process leading to end products. Thus, central office administrators and supervisors must acknowledge that teachers' growth occurs over time and requires both support and challenge as teachers engage in complex new experiences in their schools. As Alan J. Reiman and Lois Thies-Sprinthall point out, when supervisors become more skilled at guiding teachers in reflection, they foster such development.

SALARY AND FRINGE BENEFITS

Salary data for central office jobs as directors, managers, coordinators, and supervisors are broken out for the broad areas of finance and business, instructional services, public relations/information, staff personnel services, and subject area supervisors. Data for other areas, including pupil personnel, research, food services, health, transportation, federal programs, media services, and plant operations, are lumped together. Information on salaries for many types of positions within these various categories is lost in the generalizing of data for broad areas. The data are made even more vague by being reported as means. On the positive side, the figures give a clear indication of the salary that can generally be expected for certain categories of personnel.

The scheduled salaries of directors, managers, and coordinators vary according to the size and the per-pupil expenditure of the school districts. Table 4.1 shows the mean of average salaries paid to various categories of central office personnel, by school district enrollment. More specific data are available from the Educational Research Service in Arlington, Virginia.

As the table indicates, the means for administrators and supervisors are highest in districts with 25,000 students or more. The mean in districts with 25,000 students or more averages about $8,749 more than the mean in districts with 10,000 to 24,999 students. The latter mean, in turn, averages $4,589 more than the mean in districts with 2,500 to 9,999 students. And the latter mean averages $11,460 more than the mean in districts with 300 to 2,499 students.

As Table 4.1 also shows, among central office personnel (excluding superintendents, associate superintendents, and assistant superintendents), in districts with 25,000 students or more, the position with the highest mean is the administrator for finance and business. In districts with 2,500 to 24,999 students, the position with the highest mean is the administrator for instructional services. In districts with 300 to 2,499 students, the position with the highest mean is the administrator for staff personnel services.

Table 4.1 Mean of Average Salaries Paid to Central Office Personnel (in Dollars), by School District Enrollment, 2002

	Systems of 25,000 or More Students	Systems of 10,000–24,999 Students	Systems of 2,500–9,999 Students	Systems of 300–2,499 Students
Administrator for				
Finance and business	95,214	84,373	78,853	61,851
Instructional services	93,377	85,473	79,287	65,139
Public relations/information	81,670	65,147	54,654	53,874
Staff personnel services	90,543	83,959	77,904	70,489
Technology	91,051	77,500	69,176	50,933
Subject area supervisor	69,082	63,952	68,456	56,408
Other administrative staff	62,917	62,203	62,754	51,571

Source: Adapted from *Measuring Changes in Salaries and Wages in Public Schools* (2002 ed.), by Educational Research Service, 2002, Arlington, VA: Author.

Table 4.2 Mean Gain in Average Salaries Paid to Central Office Personnel (in Dollars), by School District Enrollment, 1996 and 2002

	Systems of 25,000 or More Students	Systems of 10,000–24,999 Students	Systems of 2,500–9,999 Students	Systems of 300–2,499 Students
Average salary				
1996	65,635	62,634	60,996	52,943
2002	83,407	74,658	70,069	58,609
Average gain	17,772	12,024	9,073	5,666
Percentage gain based on 1996 data	+27%	+19%	+14.87%	+10.70%

Source: From *Measuring Changes in Salaries and Wages in Public Schools* (1996 and 2002 eds.), by Educational Research Service, 1996, 2002, Arlington, VA: Author.

Not surprisingly, the data include a new role type under administration—technology—and in districts with 25,000 students or more, the mean for this administrator is among the highest—$91,051.

Table 4.2 shows mean gains in average salaries paid to central office personnel since 1996, by school district enrollment. In districts with 25,000 students or more, the mean gain was $17,772, or 27 percent; in districts with 10,000 to 24,999 students, $12,024, or 19 percent; in districts with 2,500 to 9,999 students, $9,073, or about 15 percent; and in districts with 300 to 2,499 students, $5,666, or about 11 percent. Obviously, salary increases are staying ahead of inflation (which averages about 3 percent per year) in districts with 10,000 students or more.

Fringe benefits for central office administrators and supervisors, including those at the building level, are the same as those for principals and assistant principals. They are reported in Chapter 3.

FIRSTHAND ACCOUNT

Paul Keene is the director of professional development for the Granville County Schools, whose headquarters are in Oxford, North Carolina. He has been an educator since 1977, when he graduated from Colgate University. He holds a master's degree in curriculum and instruction (with an emphasis on supervision) from North Carolina State University, where he is currently pursuing a Ph.D. in curriculum and instruction. He describes how he got started in central office administration, what the work is like, what some of the upsides and downsides are, and what he would advise people aspiring to a position like his.

Like many successful teachers and administrators, I grew up in an education family—both of my parents are educators. After two years of graduate study in French literature, I moved to North Carolina, where I taught Latin and French in a private day school for three years before moving to the public schools. Some years into the ensuing twelve-year stint teaching French in a small rural high school, I was invited to become a mentor for new teachers. Soon I was the mentor trainer for my small (8,000-student) system, running an intensive fifteen-week class to prepare veteran teachers to help new teachers.

My role as advocate for proper support and conditions for new teachers continued to grow, as did the number of new teachers in our district. In 1996 I was invited to move to the central office to become the system's first coordinator of services to initially licensed teachers. This was a half-time position. My other challenge was to create an English-as-a-second-language program for the few immigrant students who were beginning to appear in our schools.

Since that time the English-as-a-second-language program has grown from 30 students to 400. Also, my responsibilities have expanded to include the lead role in the district's Total Quality Education initiative, director of the migrant education program, and director of staff development. (I like to say that I have five half-time jobs!) I also returned part time to graduate school, where I earned a master's degree in supervision.

I see my job as a service one, with teachers and principals as my customers. My mission is to help them be as successful as possible in promoting student achievement. Much of my professional life is focused on adult learners since I organize, facilitate, and actually teach a lot of professional development for teachers and administrators. It takes plenty of planning and preparation to make sure that these experiences are worthwhile for people who already are busy doing important work.

The area of professional learning integrates all my disparate duties. I see it as the core of my job and a great opportunity to move my system closer to being a learning organization. It also means that my days are long, as many sessions are late in the day or in the evening.

Meetings, for better or for worse, are a big part of life in the central office. As well as attending the meetings of the various teams and committees on which I serve, I am responsible for leading a whole suite of meetings, representing all my "hats." Some of these are monthly meetings that include more than sixty principals, teachers, and administrators. It takes a lot of preparation time to make sure that these meetings have clear and appropriate outcomes, workable agendas, powerful visuals, and handouts and resources.

We have recently moved to an online registration system for staff development. I am the resource person whenever there is a problem.

I also represent my district at meetings around the state. The more hats you wear, the more such meetings you will attend. Although this takes up precious time, I enjoy the variety, the change of scenery, and the networking opportunities. Sometimes serving school-based educators means giving them bad news or unpleasant tasks. As state and federal mandates and program requirements become more complex, central office staffers are called on to ensure compliance and to ask schools for the data for required reports. I work hard to build strong relationships so that these efforts are not resented.

Upsides and Downsides

The biggest reward of my job is the sense that I am making a difference. Some of our professional learning initiatives have made our organization a better place to work and to learn. On the other hand, I have to face the fact that much improvement is outside my direct influence. Each school, controlled by the faculty and especially the principal, has a unique culture and is the primary unit of educational reform. Central office administrators can only encourage, inform, and advocate in support of school reform.

I am in a position to keep a big-picture orientation. I don't know everything that's going on, but I have a sense of how things fit together and can see the alignment of programs, initiatives, and concerns at the classroom, school, district, state, and federal levels. This helps me in conversations with teachers, as I can help them contextualize their questions and concerns.

I enjoy the variety and the flexibility of my job. Every day is different, and I decide how to structure my time as I move among many different tasks. This kind of environment makes it very easy to stop thinking strategically and become a "task completer." When the "urgent" phone calls and E-mails pour in, it is an effort to be proactive and not let myself be pulled in a dozen directions.

Advice

If central office administration sounds like a good fit for you, the most general advice is simple: keep learning and be reflective. The appropriate graduate degree and certification are important, but you will need some other skills that may not be included in formal schooling. Be able to conduct great meetings and workshops in which people enjoy participating. Find people who can do this and ask them how they learned—get the training.

Expect your responsibilities to grow. Extra duties have a way of getting added. Think of it as a growth opportunity.

If you are ambitious, stay with school administration for a while before you try to move to the central office. Former principals have a much better chance at superintendencies. In either case, work on balancing leadership with followership skills, and on building relationships. You will enlist people by example, inspiration, persuasion, and consensus building, not by commanding.

C H A P T E R

5

SPECIAL SERVICES

Chapter 4 gives attention to specialists who work in a school district's central office or one of its regional offices. This chapter deals mainly with specialists who work at the school-building level with students, teachers, principals, other specialists, and parents. Building-level specialists include teachers and supervisors of art, music, and physical education; school library media specialists; computer specialists; school counselors; school psychologists; school social workers; reading teachers; English-as-a-second-language teachers; special education teachers; school nurses; occupational and physical therapists; and speech-language pathologists and audiologists. The information included in this chapter often applies as well to staff in central office positions who are in the same specialist categories.

Consideration of specialists is important because more specialists are being assigned to the building level as mandates and recommendations for school improvement materialize and because existing programs in most of these positions continue to have openings. Three examples of the former illustrate why there is a continuous call for specialists.

1. The Education for All Handicapped Children Act of 1975 (Public Law 94-142), which was reenacted in 1990 as the Individuals with Disabilities Education Act (Public Law 101-476) and is currently being considered for reauthorization, mandates that youngsters with disabilities receive a "free, appropriate public education that includes special education and related services to meet their unique needs," and that individualized education

programs be planned and provided for them. To implement this legislation, schools need many more specialists in school buildings than before, including occupational therapists, physical therapists, school psychologists, and school social workers.

2. Recent advances in technology, particularly in the personal computer, have required that schools employ computer and other technology experts to instruct both students and teachers. The first need is for teachers to learn how to use computers and other hardware, to become acquainted with software, and, most important, to find effective ways to use technology to enhance student learning. This requires that teachers and administrators develop new attitudes about instruction. It also calls for technicians, curriculum specialists, and supervisors to assist and support teachers.

3. The recommendation made by several national commissions that teachers be given greater authority for decision making (and thus that more autonomy be delegated to the building level) creates a need for additional specialists and support personnel, such as lead teachers, technology experts, and health care experts, to work onsite with teachers and administrators.

Some explanation regarding the third example may be helpful. Teachers and other educators who work directly with children and adolescents are in a better position to recognize the unique characteristics, problems, needs, and interests of students than administrators and specialists who are more distant. Before the recommendation to give teachers more responsibility for decision making, the goal was to have all schools in a district—in fact, all students in similar grades or subjects—cover the same curriculum. Research and experience have proved such expectations to be unrealistic. Children are sufficiently different in ability, interest, background, and attitude that a single curriculum cannot satisfy or accommodate all students. Schools that have recognized and responded to the differences in their students have been more successful than those that have laid down essentially the same expectations for all students.

To implement a program that responds to the students being taught, teachers need to fashion curriculum to their own situations. As a result, curriculum becomes different in each school, though the general goals of education for each school in the district may be the same. Strong support is apparent for such an approach. No less prestigious and influential a group than the Carnegie Task Force on Teaching as a Profession, for example, has recommended that "teachers . . . be provided with the discretion and autonomy that are the hallmarks of professional work" and that they have "the ability to make—or at least to strongly influence—decisions concerning such things as the materials and instructional method used." Carrying out such a recommendation would enable teachers to accommodate each student better. In an ideal situation, they would individualize each youngster's curriculum.

Some of the latter is probably not possible in present and near-future circumstances. The No Child Left Behind Act, passed by Congress in 2002, appears to direct schools to seek more standard achievement by students. Even though the act invites states and school districts to develop standards of adequate yearly progress, it includes provisos that students be assessed in reading and mathematics in grades 3 through 8 by 2005–06 and in science at three levels by 2007–08, and that the standards be applied to all students.

These two directions clearly appear to be in conflict. It is difficult to predict what will develop as the No Child Left Behind Act, or a modification of it, is implemented. Nonetheless, there probably will be more decision making on curriculum and instruction at the building level and in classrooms. Specialists are important in that process. Such assistance is, in fact, essential to teachers, who alone do not have the time, perspective, or expertise to diagnose, plan, teach, remedy, and evaluate all that a responsive school program requires.

As events unfold, specialists will be used differently. Exactly how their roles will be modified still is not clear, but creating the staffing patterns, the collaborative efforts, and the instructional approaches needed will involve stimulating and challenging work for specialists and school faculties.

Keeping up-to-date on specialists is simple. Each specialty has a professional association, which maintains a website that reports current information, resources, and other features of interest. See the Appendix for the various associations' website addresses.

RESPONSIBILITIES OF SPECIALISTS

Specialists in the categories named in the opening paragraph of this chapter have some common characteristics. For example, many are both teachers and consultants: they teach or counsel students directly, and they consult with teachers in their area of expertise. For art, music, and physical education specialists in elementary schools, that double duty takes the form of actually teaching classes of children as well as helping the elementary school teacher teach the subject. For all specialists, it involves working with students and consulting with teachers and other school personnel who deal with students.

Some examples may help illustrate what specialists contribute. Teachers in the elementary school often try to integrate subjects. A social studies unit, for example, may include not only the history and the geography of a country but also the country's culture—its art, dance, literature, and music. One or more specialists may help the classroom teacher create such a unit, advising on content, materials, and teaching techniques.

Another example is development of an individualized education program for a student with a disability. Special educators, school social workers, school psychologists, occupational and physical therapists, and speech-language pathologists collaborate with teachers and parents to plan a program that is appropriate for that child. The issue in special education is to determine what should be expected of a student and how various teachers and specialists—and parents—can contribute to achieving the goals on which they agree.

Another characteristic that specialists share is that in certain settings, particularly in small and medium-sized school districts, they may teach their subject at several levels. For example, specialists in art, music, physical education, and foreign language may teach classes in the elementary, junior high, and high school. In many instances that requires serving several schools and relating to the program and the teachers in each school.

Special education teachers may have their own classroom in a school. Reading specialists and speech-language pathologists frequently use smaller rooms for tutoring, remedial work, and coaching. Today, however, the expectations of the No Child Left Behind Act and the 1997 amendments to the Individuals with Disabilities Education Act are that the majority of students with disabilities be educated in regular classrooms by general education teachers, often in consultation with special education teachers and other specialists. This practice, dubbed *inclusion*, can create problems, even though it can be highly successful. It challenges teachers to individualize more, even for students without disabilities.

Depending on students' learning and behavioral needs, they may be pulled out of the classroom for short periods for diagnosis, remedial instruction, or intervention in another location. In schools that use group counseling, the school counselor may bring students together in a separate space to provide small- and large-group counseling or to form developmental groups that focus on such matters as friendship, study skills, grief, or divorce.

In all these types of assistance, the specialist consults with and advises the teacher so that each student's learning program has coherence and consistency. Increasingly, teachers and specialists strive to embed strategies in the regular school day rather than apply them in separate pull-out sessions.

Scheduling time for collaborative planning and for specialists' work can be challenging. Teachers are particularly sensitive to pull-out practices because they disrupt students' concentration and the rhythm of learning in the classroom.

School counselors, school library media specialists, school psychologists, school social workers, school nurses, occupational and physical therapists, speech-language pathologists, and audiologists act in still other capacities. The school counselor, who is present in greater numbers than the other specialists just mentioned, serves in a mode that illustrates, at least in part, the kinds of services all these specialists provide.

School counseling focuses on the academic, social-emotional, and career development of all students. Most high school counselors confer with students individually. Recently they have begun to consult more with teachers and principals, encouraging them to take a greater responsibility in guiding the personal-social adjustment of youngsters and to assume a more prominent role in advising. In the elementary school, counselors do some individual counseling, but they have long spent more time helping teachers create a better environment in which children can learn and develop.

A problem for counselors (and teachers) in all schools is confidentiality. Individual counseling probably is their most delicate activity. It involves developing trust. Students frequently reveal facts and feelings that cannot be shared. Yet counselors often consult with parents and teachers about the students whom they counsel. Discretion and good judgment therefore are important qualifications for counselors. School counselors—indeed, all helping professionals—must follow a professional code of ethics.

In large schools, several professional and support staff usually share the many duties carried on by school counselors. Increasingly, school counselors work with single parents, who in many cases are looking for solutions to problems that married couples might solve for themselves.

Providing group counseling or support groups for children of recently divorced parents is another task for school counselors.

All the foregoing services may not be available from counselors actually located in a school building. Many school districts have a full-time staff of specialists at their central office. In smaller school districts or in those that cannot afford full-time personnel in a particular specialty, such specialists are provided by cooperative service boards, intermediate school districts, or both.

KINDS OF SPECIALISTS

This chapter already has touched briefly on some of the ways in which school-level specialists assist teachers and students. Following is a more in-depth look at the responsibilities, education, and training of the more common specialists.

Art Teachers and Supervisors

In 2003 the National Art Education Association (NAEA), the primary professional association serving art teachers, reported about 22,000 members employed in public schools, colleges, and other art establishments. NAEA estimates that about 50,000 art teachers work in public schools.

In the elementary school, forty-eight states require licensure for art teachers, so art probably is taught at that level in those states. Alaska and Hawaii are the two states that do not require licensure. Art education is required in most middle and junior high schools. In grades above the sixth, it is taught by a specialist, an art teacher. In the senior high school, art usually is an elective.

In 2000, twenty-two states reported that art or fine art credits were not required for high school graduation. An NAEA study found that 11 percent of states did not count art grades when computing grade point averages. Another study found that 65 percent of universities did not count high school art grades in computing grade point averages. Obviously, the arts are not highly regarded in this era, even though students enrolled in art study score higher on the verbal and mathematics components of the Scholastic Achievement Test than students not enrolled in art study.

Teachers and supervisors of art are difficult to distinguish from one another. There are comparatively few art teachers or supervisors in the elementary school, perhaps 10,000 to 15,000. Many at this level are *itinerant teachers*—that is, they serve several schools. In the high school, teachers of art far outnumber supervisors.

Preparation for teaching art can be accomplished in four years, culminating in a bachelor's degree. An art supervisor usually must have a master's degree. In many states a master's degree or the equivalent is required for continuing certification.

The publication *Status of the States: Art Education Reports* indicates the requirements for licensure as an art teacher. Like music, art is so much a matter of experience and proficiency that subjecting all prospective art teachers to the same training makes little sense. NAEA champions this point: "Not all prospective art teachers need the same amount or even the same sequence of class work, general studies, content in the special art area, teaching and learning theory, observation/participation and practicum experience, and professional studies."

Art teachers usually are on the same salary schedule as teachers of core subjects (English, math, science, and social studies). See Chapter 2 for information about teacher salaries.

Music Teachers

About 124,600 people taught music in American public and private schools in 2002–03. This figure includes vocal and instrumental music teachers and music supervisors.

Music is usually offered as part of the overall school curriculum in the elementary, middle, and junior high school, and as an elective in the senior high school. A number of music specialists teach at more than one level.

In grades 1 through 3, music offerings tend to be general music. In grades 4 through 8, some schools also offer band, chorus, and orchestra. Instrumental and vocal music programs are part of many elementary, middle, and junior high school programs. Whether they are curricular or extracurricular is a local option. Some schools build both vocal and instrumental music into the school day. Others offer only instrumental music during school hours. Choirs, bands, and orchestras usually meet before or after school or during lunch.

Music in senior high school most often includes courses and performance groups. Schools may offer courses in general music, theory, music history, and literature. Some may offer classes in voice training. Performance groups include band, orchestra, chorus, and sometimes music theater. Some high schools have extensive offerings. Others have very lean programs.

The specialists who teach and direct these activities have various titles, such as teacher, director, or supervisor.

Beginning music teachers and supervisors in all states must have a bachelor's degree. In most states a master's degree or the equivalent is required for regular licensure.

MENC: The National Association for Music Education is the major professional association for music teachers and supervisors. As of October 2002, MENC had 54,126 active members. MENC offers several publications of interest to anyone exploring music teaching. See the Bibliography for details.

Like art teachers, music teachers typically are on the same salary schedule as teachers of core subjects (English, math, science, and social studies). See Chapter 2 for information about teacher salaries.

Physical Education Teachers

Teachers of physical education are usually considered special teachers in the elementary school. In the high school, depending on their assignment, they may or may not be designated as special teachers. Most high school physical education teachers carry the teaching load of the regular teacher. The size of the school, of course, determines more precisely how both elementary and secondary physical education teachers are designated and how they are assigned. In small districts or schools, physical education teachers may teach physical education from grades 5 through 12 in one or several schools. In large schools, they may have a full-time assignment in a single school.

In middle, junior high, and senior high schools, physical education teachers and classes are becoming integrated by sex. In the elementary schools, men or women always have taught boys and girls together. Instruction includes exercises, games, dance of various kinds, and good sports behavior.

In the elementary school, physical education also is recreation. Young children have difficulty being confined to a desk in a classroom. Sports and games with the physical education teacher, in addition to having learning value, are a chance to let off steam.

High school physical education focuses more on physical development and sports. Teachers give tests to determine students' development and fitness at particular ages.

At either level the physical education teacher also may teach classes in health. In the elementary or middle school, the physical education teacher may team-teach health with the classroom teacher, teach the subject alone, or serve as a consultant to the classroom teacher. A health class in the middle, junior high, or senior high school may be an academic course.

Physical education teachers also coach intramural and interscholastic sports and dance at any level, although interscholastic sports usually do not begin until high school. Intramural sports may take place during school hours. For interscholastic sports, practice usually occurs after school, and games are in the afternoon or the evening. Coaching after school is usually an additional duty for which physical education teachers receive extra pay. Varsity coaches often are hired for their coaching ability, and teaching physical education classes is a secondary responsibility, or at least thought to be. Often a varsity coach has a lighter classroom teaching load.

To begin teaching in public schools, teachers and special teachers in physical education are required to complete a bachelor's degree and be certified by the state. They are on the same salary schedule as regular teachers (see Chapter 2).

School Library Media Specialists

More than 75,000 school librarians/media professionals work in the public schools. School library media specialists are a comparatively new breed, and computer specialists in this area are even newer. They work in places that keep print, recorded, photographed, audiovisual, and other materials and have names like *school library*, *learning resource center*, *instructional materials center*, and *library/media center*. The names vary because of the explosion in both the kinds of information and other resources that can be stored and retrieved, and the forms and the ways in which those resources are managed.

The transition is far from complete. Libraries and media centers still are in the midst of change. As the demand for and the use of audiovisual equipment, computers, and technology resources have become greater, as their quantity and quality have increased, and as their accessibility has improved, they have been integrated into the other resources of the library. For example, a book and a map depicting the life and the geography of India now can be supplemented by films or CD-ROMs showing the Indian people in their habitat. With the Internet accessible in schools, students and teachers have access to resources on websites and in databases. With E-mail they can communicate with fellow students throughout the world.

The use of computers is progressing at a dazzling pace. For example, in only a few years, many schools have computerized their library card catalogs, and that change is inevitable—even imminent—for almost all schools. Databases, from which information is retrieved by telecommunication on personal computers, are developing with enormous speed. When equipment becomes generally available in schools and students learn how to use it, they will gain access to databases and other electronic sources.

Whereas *librarian* formerly meant strictly that, today it means *library media specialist* and more. The labels of state licenses in the field indicate the confusion and the difference of opinion on this specialist's role: school librarian, media generalist, librarian/media specialist, instructional media specialist, materials or media specialist, and audiovisual librarian. Anyone considering a career in this specialty should inquire about developments in the field, explore the curricula being offered at colleges preparing such personnel, and investigate the most enlightened programs before selecting a place to study.

Jobs as a library media specialist vary greatly, influenced by the size of the school, the degree to which media and technology have been integrated, and the school district's concept of materials and technology support. Of course, the emphasis and the support given to the maintenance and the use of a comprehensive resource center also are important. Without a highly qualified specialist on a faculty, a library or media center is little more than a repository for learning resources.

School library media specialists perform many demanding tasks. In addition to handling all the management functions—selecting, ordering, and processing items—they work with teachers in finding and organizing materials, developing curricula, and preparing units for teaching. They must be well versed in the library or media center's holdings and particularly cognizant of materials appropriate for the age level of the students they serve. If access to resources via technology is a service of the center, personnel must have appropriate competencies.

Library media specialists also orient students in the use of the library or media center and assist them in finding materials. Some are expert in storytelling, graphics, photography, filming, videotaping, or electronic databases. Many library media specialists teach, and some team-teach with teachers.

Where computers are available (see the next section on computer specialists), the library media specialist must not only be knowledgeable about their use but also know how to help others use them. This may mean assisting people in overcoming a fear of computers, often more prevalent among teachers than students.

The work of library media specialists is highly professional. Nearly all states require them to be licensed. Forty-nine states require a teacher's credential as well as a specialist's, particularly for the regular license (essentially a permanent license).

The master's degree in library science, media science, or library media science, historically obtainable in one year of study beyond the bachelor's degree, is increasingly demanding more time because of the additional competencies that the position requires. In the near future, the master's degree will probably be required in most states. The American Association of School Librarians (AASL; a department of the American Library Association) and the Association for Educational Communications and Technology (AECT), in their joint standards for training and certification (last released in 1988, now being revised), recommend the master's degree as the entry-level requirement. Each association also has recommendations regarding training for specialists in its area. People interested in library media careers in schools are advised to contact these associations for advice.

Many school library media specialists work essentially the same number of hours as teachers. However, some are classified as administrators because they oversee a large enterprise and a number of professional, technical, and nonprofessional personnel (secretaries and student and adult aides). The school year of these specialists may be longer than that of teachers because they must organize at the end of the year and prepare for the beginning of a new year. Selecting, ordering, and processing material sometimes creates summer employment for library media specialists, particularly in larger schools. Library media administrators often are on twelve-month appointments and are classified with administrators and supervisors for purposes of salary and other benefits (see Chapter 3).

The job market for library media specialists is stable and increasing. People interested in the field should seek part-time, work-study, or volunteer work in a library or media center. When such experience occurs before training, the prospective specialist has an opportunity to view firsthand the nature and conditions of work and to gain an impression of the competence required. When such experience takes place during training, the prospective specialist gains an advantage over other candidates at employment time.

The mean salary for library media specialists in 2002–03 was $43,320, according to the Bureau of Labor Statistics. The Educational Research Service reports that in 2001–02 the range of salaries for librarians was $39,335 to $56,573.

Computer Specialists

Originally the computer specialist in a school was a self-trained person with an interest in computers and other technology. More and more in recent years, though, computer specialists, including school computer specialists, have gone through organized training programs in colleges and universities or other organizations and agencies.

To help veteran education personnel (teachers and college professors) become computer literate and to help them stay current in the rapidly developing field of technology in teaching, user groups, colleges and universities, and other agencies offer study in computer technology and literacy. The early emphasis on programming and the inner workings of the computer has shifted to a focus on computer use and facility with software. A major change in all computer professional development has been a shift from learning about technology to learning from technology.

Originally, most people used the computer for word processing. As technology has expanded and as teachers and others have become computer literate, external dimensions to computer use have developed, including communication and information. At first, such dimensions were possible only through dial-up connections (via modems) over regular telephone lines. In recent years, people have had access to DSLs (digital subscriber lines), cable, T-1 lines (dedicated telephone lines), and wireless connections. These have increased transmission speeds ten to fifty times that possible on a dial-up connection.

The Internet now provides contact with people and databases all over the world. Anyone with the equipment, the software, and access to a server can send and receive information and images with a computer. This new tool for learning and for transmission at lightning speed obviously is a gold mine for teachers, students, and schools.

Professional development for specialists (and teachers) has expanded greatly in the last ten years, with training programs now provided by software and hardware companies, colleges and universities, and numerous professional organizations. As a result of National Council for Accreditation of Teacher Education standards, new teachers are coming into the profession with more sophistication in technology, particularly in the use of computers.

Many school computer specialists, with support from the federal government through Preparing Tomorrow's Teachers for Using Technology, have provided new and veteran teachers with training in computer use and in the use of computers for instruction. Despite these efforts, some teachers still use technology in traditional ways—for drill and practice in basic skills. However, efforts to support student-centered approaches to instruction are receiving major prominence today so that students can conduct their own inquiry while the teacher serves as facilitator or coach.

Defining the place and the role of the computer specialist is complicated further because of several approaches being tried to bring computers and other technology into use in schools. Whether a computer specialist should teach computer use or consult on computers, or knowledgeable teachers should tutor colleagues in using the computer in teaching, is an open question. A major problem is the fear of computers among the present generation of teachers. To reduce fear and encourage use, a program to recruit a cadre of computer-literate teachers to tutor colleagues was recently initiated. The program already is operational in a number of school districts.

As yet, computer specialists have no established home base in the organization of a school, and they may never have one. The preceding description identifies some roles for computer specialists in teaching and teacher education. They also are found on the staffs of libraries and media centers, probably because the technology fits so well with materials, media, and equipment, and because the computer can be helpful in cataloging. Further, they serve as central office consultants, visiting schools to advise, conduct workshops, and sometimes teach students directly. In the central office itself, the value of the computer in number crunching has given specialists a role in school finance. Finally, most school districts have a website that requires constant attention. This need has created the job of webmaster.

State education departments are beginning to establish policies on the competence needed for a credential in computer technology. Most states promote integration of technology into the curriculum, and a little more than half of them require computer training for new teachers. However, the use of computers in schools, and the training for such use, are not far enough advanced at this writing that states have established licensure in the field.

Anyone interested in becoming a computer specialist should seek information from the Association for Educational Communications and Technology, the American Association of School Librarians, library media departments and personal computer centers in their local community or at nearby universities, computer user groups, and electronic bulletin boards.

In 2001, more than 493,200 computer specialists worked in many settings, in schools and elsewhere. Their average salary was $41,920.

School Counselors

There are more than 200,000 education, vocational, and school counselors in private practice, government, business, and education. Counselors in the nation's public elementary and secondary schools represent the largest single group in this specialty, numbering almost 96,000.

School counselors are concerned with helping students understand themselves and the world around them better. To do so effectively, they must be a part of a school counseling program that is comprehensive in scope, preventive in design, and developmental in nature. In the words of an American School Counselor Association publication:

> The purpose of a counseling program in a school setting is to promote and enhance the learning process. To that end, the School Counseling Program facilitates Student Development in three broad areas: Academic Development, Career Development, and Personal/ Social Development.

School counselors work with teachers, principals, other school personnel, and parents to help students. They may observe a student in the classroom to advise the teacher on possible ways to deal more effectively with the child. When the difficulty is beyond the expertise of the teacher, they counsel the child.

Looking more closely at what school counselors do reveals a multitude of other duties. In general, they ensure that student records are maintained according to state and federal regulations; assist students with academic program planning; and collect, maintain, and share up-to-date occupational, educational, personal, and social information on students. Responsibilities may include interpreting cognitive, aptitude, and achievement tests; counseling students who are frequently tardy or absent; collaborating with teachers to present guidance curriculum lessons; counseling students with a discipline problem; analyzing grade point averages in relationship to achievement; interpreting student records; providing teachers with classroom management suggestions; helping school administrators identify and resolve student issues, needs, and problems; and analyzing school and counseling program data to measure effectiveness.

School counselors also arrange special programs, such as college and career days, and help students become aware of educational and career opportunities. In high school they advise students about available loans and scholarships; stay informed about and in touch with colleges, universities, and other postsecondary institutions; and assist students in finding appropriate employment (part-time, summer, and postschool).

Counselors who serve junior high and middle schools do more individual counseling than those in elementary schools. They also promote other mechanisms for guidance and advisement, such as homeroom. More and more, counselors encourage teachers to consult with students on both academic and personal-social problems.

Counselors of all sorts are linked together by the American Counselor Association (ACA). This 55,000-member organization is the umbrella group for seventeen divisions serving different types of counselors and human development specialists.

ACA maintains two services of special interest to anyone exploring a career in counseling: information on approved institutions for preparation and data on employment opportunities. The American School Counselor Association, the division of ACA specifically for school counselors or those interested in the profession, has 13,000 members. To hold a professional membership in this organization, a person must have earned a master's degree or higher in counseling and either be credentialed as a school counselor by a state, district, or territory; be employed as a school counselor or supervisor; or be employed as a counselor educator in a graduate program. Affiliate, retired, and student memberships also are available.

Most school counselors work the same school year as teachers. A few have contracts of ten-and-one-half or eleven months. A school counselor's salary depends on length of service, level of preparation, size of school district, and per-pupil expenditure. In 1999–2000, the average salary was $41,724. School counselors on the central office staff often are on a salary schedule different from that of school counselors at the building level (see Chapter 4).

School Psychologists

School psychologists work in educational settings, largely in schools. They team with teachers and other school personnel and with parents and other mental health professionals. Their goal is to ensure that every child learns in a safe, healthy, supportive environment. They consult with teachers and other educators to help develop environments that promote the intellectual, social, and emotional growth of students. They work with school faculty members to fashion programs for youngsters with disabilities, to devise strategies for dealing with disruptive students, and to deal with crisis management. They provide inservice education for teachers and other school personnel.

School psychologists also consult with teachers, parents, and administrators in finding healthy, effective alternatives to problems with learning and behavior, and they help strengthen relationships with the adults with whom students work. Assessment of student growth and development is one of the core services that school psychologists provide. They assess, or help other school personnel assess, students' academic skills, learning aptitudes, personality, social skills, and emotional development. They consult with teachers in interpreting standardized test scores, fathoming students' attitudes and motivations, and understanding the cultural backgrounds of their charges.

School psychologists work with students and teachers during their own visits to schools or during students' or teachers' visits to a student personnel center in a school district's central office.

To be a school psychologist, a candidate must complete a minimum of sixty graduate semester hours and a yearlong internship. A large percentage of school psychologists, however, have Ph.D. degrees. Both preparations emphasize mental health, learning, motivation, child behavior and development, and school organization.

The National Association of School Psychologists (NASP), with more than 23,000 members, is the primary professional association serving school psychologists. The American Psychological Association (APA) also serves school psychologists; however, only about 1,600 of its members practice in schools. It recognizes a role for school psychologists with master's-level preparation, in supervised work within an organized setting. NASP standards are more in line with those of state departments of education. Most states require state licensure to practice in schools. However, requirements vary. Aspirants for school psychologist positions should consult the *NASDTEC Manual on Preparation and Certification of Educational Personnel*, which lists requirements for each of the fifty states and Canada. It is published annually (see the Bibliography).

Actually, two types of licensure are available for school psychologists, one required and the other optional (in the school context). The state license is required by law. The school psychologist with a doctorate may seek certification from the state examining board for psychology. The latter is essential only if the psychologist engages in independent, unsupervised practice. For school psychologists who have secondary employment in private practice, this certification is obligatory.

There are two professional associations to which school psychologists might belong. NASP exists exclusively for school psychologists and admits master's-level practitioners to full membership, as well as those with a master's degree plus thirty hours and those with a doctorate. APA includes all types of psychologists and is larger (about 150,000 members). APA restricts full membership to those with an earned doctorate in psychology.

A list of state examining boards for psychology is available from APA. State boards are a source of information on the status of institutions offering graduate training and on state requirements for practice. APA also disseminates a list of institutions accredited for doctoral-level study in the practice specialties of psychology, school psychology among them.

Salaries for school psychologists depend on level of preparation, years of experience, size of school district, and per-pupil expenditure. A 1999 study by NASP reported the mean national salary for full-time school psychologists to be $49,089; for full-time school psychologists with a master's degree plus thirty semester hours, $49,738; and for full-time school psychologists with a doctorate, $55,262.

School Social Workers

Employment of school social workers is growing across the nation, with more than 15,000 such positions scattered across the country. Although certification standards differ from state to state, most school social workers hold a Master of Social Work (MSW), which prepares them to work with students, families, and school staff.

School social workers are committed to providing better assurance that teachers have teachable children. Their purpose is to help students (and teachers and families) when psychosocial factors interfere with students' adjustment to school or when problems develop in the interaction of students' characteristics and the school's policies and practices. For example, a student may blatantly and persistently violate the expectations of the school by lying, stealing, threatening violence, being tardy or absent, using inappropriate or obscene language, cheating on school work, or showing gross disrespect for other students or the teacher. The student's teacher and the principal may suspect that the behavior is the result of such factors as conflict between home and school, severe social discomfort, poor mental health, or cultural differences, and they may call on the school social worker to evaluate, consult, and intervene (or take other appropriate action).

Intervention often is guided by a team of specialists, including the teacher, to bring a wide array of expertise to analyze and diagnose the problem. Frequently, families are involved in discussions of remedies. The team devises a plan to alter the interaction of the school, the community, and the student's characteristics. The social worker may involve community-based social workers to ensure that the resources are in play to make the school, the community, and the student more compatible. The purpose is to find the most effective intervention to bring about a change in one or more of those three variables so that the student will have the opportunity to take charge of his or her own learning and development.

School social workers must have a wide array of talents, abilities, and skills. They must be able to conduct interviews, establish and maintain purposeful relationships, observe and assess circumstances, collect appropriate information, evaluate influences operating in school-community-family relationships, determine and apply the most appropriate methods and techniques, collaborate with team members and community agencies, consult with people in the client system, maintain liaison between a student's home and school, implement referrals to resources, identify and develop resources, coordinate interdisciplinary efforts, develop curriculum, assess intervention, and more. New trends in school social work include working with groups or classrooms of students. School social workers excel in developing social skills, peer mediation skills, and conflict resolution skills. Clearly, school social workers can play a role in the nationwide focus of making all schools safe and eliminating bullying.

The National Association of Social Workers (NASW) and the School Social Work Association of America (SSWAA) recommend the MSW as the entry-level degree for school social workers. Increasingly, state boards of education are establishing minimum standards for these personnel. Currently, about half of the states regulate school social workers, and most of them require the MSW for full licensure. SSWAA provides career information and sponsors annual conferences for school social workers.

Salaries for school social workers are comparable to those for school psychologists and school counselors.

Reading Teachers

One of the popular clichés in schools is that every teacher is a teacher of reading. That probably is true, but some teachers specialize in reading. They are licensed to work with students from kindergarten through grade 12. Typically they teach and tutor children in the elementary school—and sometimes in middle or junior high school—who are below grade level in reading. These often are deprived or disadvantaged children, or those with learning disabilities.

Reading specialists often begin by administering a diagnostic test to determine the student's reading difficulty. This usually includes attention to reading, writing, speaking, and listening because of their natural relationship. Reading specialists then interpret the results and prescribe remedial work to improve a youngster's literacy skills. They may take children from the regular classroom during the school day to conduct remedial work. This approach is called a *pull-out program*. The emphasis may be on such skills as decoding and phonics, but it also may encompass a broader approach to improvement in literacy.

Reading specialists support their efforts by conferring with the regular classroom teachers to build continuity and reinforcement in the approaches used to improve a youngster's literacy. The reading specialist and the classroom teacher, who may have special preparation in teaching literacy, often work from different materials, so ensuring continuity and fostering the integration of classroom and special assistance are essential. Reading specialists also consult frequently with parents on giving help and encouragement at home.

When there is time, reading specialists may work with high-achieving children for enrichment purposes. Five- or six-year-olds who are advanced in language development often need special attention, support, and encouragement to stay interested because the regular pace of instruction in the classroom becomes monotonous and boring to them.

The trend in the rhetoric on reading, and on literacy in general, seems to be away from a hard-driving emphasis on mechanics and basic readers toward a wider use of children's literature, development of an interest in reading, and creation of relationships between a child's reading, writing, speaking, and listening. However, practice and public pressure still are focused on developing reading skills, pure and simple, with a primary goal of improving test scores. The No Child Left Behind Act appears to have that emphasis.

One sign of a broadening view is the development of an emphasis on children's reading and the relationship of writing to reading. Computers often are used as part of such an approach. For example, the teacher may employ computer programs that enable the student to proceed at his or her own pace. Such programs are self-correcting and include built-in rewards.

Many classroom teachers have completed courses in language arts and reading in their undergraduate programs, and an estimated 25 percent of elementary school teachers have a reading endorsement on their license. Reading specialists are prepared at the master's level, usually after they have earned a bachelor's degree, received licensure in elementary or secondary education, and acquired teaching experience. The International Reading Association (IRA) recommends that the master's degree program include several advanced courses, including basic reading and language arts, children's literature, assessment, and developmentally appropriate literacy. Certification as a reading teacher or a reading specialist is usually represented by an endorsement on a regular teaching license.

IRA offers inservice education and a host of other resources for classroom teachers, reading teachers, teacher educators, and others who teach reading.

The reading teacher may be on the regular-teacher salary schedule (see Chapter 2) or an administrative salary schedule (see Chapter 3). Applicants for such positions should inquire about salary and salary schedule before signing a contract.

English-as-a-Second-Language (ESL) Teachers

According to the most recently available national data, 2.1 million students, or 5 percent of the total school enrollment, received limited-English-proficiency services in the 1993–94 school year. State-by-state data for the 2000–01 school year showed nearly 2.3 million students receiving these services in the Mexican-border states alone: California, 1,479,819 (24.5 percent); Arizona, 131,933 (15.0 percent); New Mexico, 68,679 (21.4 percent); and Texas, 570,453 (14.1 percent). The figure continues to grow as large numbers of immigrants settle in the United States.

The main problem that the children of immigrants face in school is acquisition of adequate language skills to catch up with their native-English-speaking classmates. Opportunities for ESL teachers exist at the elementary and secondary school levels as well as in adult education, community and four-year colleges and universities, and private language centers. Many ESL teachers work abroad in various settings.

For the most part, the need for ESL teachers in the United States is focused in the regions with the highest concentration of immigrants, refugees, and other non-English-speaking residents: southern California,

San Francisco, Hawaii, Texas, Florida, New York, New Jersey, North Carolina, and other urban areas. Throughout the United States, though, universities at both the undergraduate and the graduate level, and private language centers, offer intensive ESL programs to foreign students who must perfect their language skills to qualify for admission.

In addition to providing English-language instruction to non-English-speaking students, ESL teachers develop curriculum, write materials, and conduct research. Several special-interest sections exist within the profession, such as computer-assisted language learning, video applications, program administration, and teaching of English to students with hearing impairments.

A bachelor's degree is the minimum qualification. Courses of study may include the grammatical, phonological, and semantic systems of the English language; methodology; second-language assessment; practice teaching; and the study of another language and its culture.

Master's degrees in TESOL (teaching English to speakers of other languages) and linguistics are offered by many universities. A master's degree can pave the way for administrative responsibilities and is usually the basic requirement for teaching ESL at universities at home and abroad.

TESOL, Inc. (Teachers of English to Speakers of Other Languages) has about 14,000 members. It provides access to professional development and employment opportunities.

The median annual wage of the broad category to which English-as-a-second-language teachers belong—teachers of adult literacy, remedial education, and GED (general education diploma)—was $35,220 in 2001. The Bureau of Labor Statistics expects employment opportunities for English-as-a-second-language teachers to be very good in the first decade of the twenty-first century because of the increasing number of immigrants and the growing number of those who are seeking classes.

Special Education Teachers

About 386,000 teachers in the United States work with children who have disabilities. Around 93 percent of them are employed in schools that serve students with disabilities from ages six through twenty-one.

In 1999–2000, 5.7 million children were served in federally supported programs for students with disabilities. That number broke down by disability as follows:

- Specific learning disabilities—2,900,000
- Speech or language impairment—1,100,000
- Mental retardation—613,000
- Serious emotional disturbance—469,000
- Hearing impairments—72,000
- Orthopedic impairments—71,000
- Other health impairments—254,000
- Visual impairments—27,000
- Multiple disabilities—112,000
- Deafness and blindness—1,800
- Preschool disabled—587,000

This breakdown does not include children who are gifted and talented. Those who are gifted and talented and those who have disabilities are frequently referred to collectively as *exceptional children* or *underserved, at-risk students.*

Special education teachers work in a variety of settings in schools, including specially equipped classrooms, ordinary classrooms, resource rooms, therapy rooms, clinics, and small seminar rooms. The size of the school district often determines how students with disabilities are grouped for instruction. Age separations in special education are not as rigid as in the regular (graded) classroom. Also, teachers may teach a group of children with different disabilities or multiple disabilities.

Instruction is individualized as much as possible because the children's abilities and disabilities are so different, but it always is based on the standards of the general curriculum for all students. Teachers use their understanding of how students learn to determine how a particular student learns best. The challenge is to devise an individualized education program (IEP) for each child, to find methods and materials that will achieve learning goals, to provide for the behavioral accompaniments to a particular student's disability, and, when possible, to orchestrate activities that a group can do together.

With the introduction of inclusion, special education teachers increasingly serve less of the day as teachers of children with disabilities and more as consultants to regular teachers who are instructing students with disabilities included in their classrooms. A system has evolved that teams the special educator with other service personnel, such as the school nurse, the school counselor, the school psychologist, and the principal, to focus on planning and evaluating IEPs. The special education teacher has the tasks of instructing and supporting the student, documenting his or her progress, and preparing the administrative paperwork required by federal legislation. In a professional assignment that already is intense and pressure laden, many special education teachers find the paperwork and the time that it takes stressful. At the same time, they find it rewarding to teach students with disabilities and report on their achievements.

In addition to students with physical and intellectual impairments, the special education teacher works with students who behave inappropriately, who are hyperactive or unable to attend to instruction, who have health-related disabilities that require medical support, or who have autism or other disabilities that make social relationships and communication difficult.

The use of technology in special education deserves some discussion. Teachers use computers extensively as tools for learning and as a means of providing individualized instruction. They also use computers as aids in information management, record keeping, and other administrative tasks.

Special education for gifted and talented students involves service to a very different type of underserved learner. Gifted students may appear to be regular students who are different only because they have significantly above-average intelligence, greater creative abilities, or both. Gifted students may, however, be withdrawn, precocious, self-impressed, or hyperactive. As a consequence, the task becomes not just one of teaching students who are different but also one of accommodating students whose behavior may be as confounding as that of students with disabilities.

There also is the difficulty of determining what is meant by *gifted and talented* or *underserved*. Is an overachieving or culturally privileged student gifted? Is giftedness a matter of degree? Teachers and administrators must decide at what point in a continuum of giftedness a student qualifies for a special program and then determine how to explain that decision to parents.

Teaching gifted students is a demanding assignment. It goes well beyond planning curriculum and instruction, to challenging the capabilities of students with exceptional talents and intellects. This is an area in which the teacher confers with a number of specialists, taps several opinions in assessing students' abilities, consults with others on the content and the strategy for teaching, seeks help in finding appropriate materials, and looks for assistance in evaluating progress and outcomes.

The emotional and intellectual energy required to work with exceptional children is enormous. A reassuring note is that while special education teachers consider their work stressful, they also consider themselves able to manage.

Preparation for special education is very much like preparation for other teaching specialties, except that the focus is on disabilities or giftedness. In some states, prospective special education teachers must first be licensed as elementary or secondary school teachers and then meet requirements for an emphasis in special education, such as teaching children who have hearing impairments or teaching children who are gifted. In other states, teachers may study and be licensed in several exceptionalities, usually related areas. Preparation takes at least four years of collegiate work, often more. Many teacher educators in special education recommend five years of training.

Special education teachers typically are on the regular-teacher salary schedule (see Chapter 2).

School Nurses

Of the thousands of school nurses in the nation, 12,000 belong to the National Association of School Nurses (NASN). Most school nurses are employed by school districts full-time, a few part-time.

School nurses perform a variety of services, depending on level of training, size of school district, state requirements, and other factors. Nurses are integral members of school communities. To serve a wide variety of students safely and effectively, the school nurse requires a breadth of clinical knowledge and skills, but the many differences in state requirements cause numerous variables in the services that nurses can legally provide.

NASN reports the following examples of direct services provided by school nurses:

- Health education for students, families, and staff
- Health counseling, including referrals and follow-up
- Age-appropriate health screenings, referrals, and follow-up

- Assistance in management of health conditions through individualized school health care plans
- Emergency services, such as triage and injury care
- Case management, particularly for children with special health care needs
- Community assessment of resources available to students, families, and staff

Most school nurses are committed to a wellness approach, promoting prevention rather than practicing remediation.

Since the passage of the Education for All Handicapped Children Act and its successor, the Individuals with Disabilities Education Act, school nurses have spent more time consulting with teachers and other school personnel than they did before. Children with disabilities often have health problems as well as disabilities. In fact, a health problem often causes a disability. Nurses serve as members of teams consisting of teachers, special education teachers, administrators, other allied health workers, school social workers, psychologists, parents, and others, that plan IEPs for children with disabilities.

School nurses also consult on and assist with cases of teenage pregnancy and child abuse. They help teachers in classrooms in health matters. Registered nurses (RNs) teach health and fitness courses and collaborate with other health professionals to promote preventive care. They engage in AIDS education, promoting better understanding of the virus and the way in which it is acquired. Some school nurses serve as administrators, overseeing the school nurses in a school district.

Preparation for school nursing varies considerably because of the diversity in requirements from state to state. Most school nurses are RNs. Most RNs are prepared in two-, three-, or four-year postsecondary programs. Some have earned a master's degree or a Ph.D. Many states require school nurses to be certified, and most states require them to have a bachelor's degree. A few states require school nurses to have both a nurse's license and a teacher's license.

The American School Health Association and the American Nurses Association also serve school nurses, but NASN is the only organization concerned exclusively with school nurses.

Nurses consider work in schools attractive employment. For the school nurses who work part-time, the prospect of fringe benefits is dim. Full-time nurses have the insurance, leave, and retirement benefits in their designated category, teacher or administrator/supervisor. In 2001–02 the mean of average salaries for full-time school nurses was $38,221.

Occupational Therapists

Occupational therapy in schools is designed to enable students to function effectively in the school environment. It is a related service made available to help students benefit from the special education program. Students with disabilities who qualify for special education may receive occupational therapy services in schools that are supported by state or federal funds.

The enactment of the Education for All Handicapped Children Act, and subsequently the Individuals with Disabilities Education Act (and amendments), has made schools one of the three most frequent workplaces (along with hospitals and skilled nursing facilities) for occupational therapists. In 2000 more than one-quarter of the 100,000 occupational therapy practitioners in the nation worked in schools or other settings with children.

The occupational therapist in schools may have one or more of three functions:

1. Assessment and evaluation, or identifying a child's strengths and weaknesses in self-care skills and determining the skills that he or she needs to improve in order to function effectively in school
2. Consultation, or helping the IEP team plan a child's treatment
3. Intervention, or directly providing occupational therapy services

Some schools employ occupational therapists directly. Others contract with outside agencies for occupational therapy services. In such instances, children often are bused to hospitals or other facilities for treatment.

Forty-six states and the District of Columbia require occupational therapists to be licensed. Forty-three states require occupational therapy assistants to be licensed. The license is issued by a special licensure board, different in each state but usually made up of occupational therapists, occupational therapy assistants, consumer members, and sometimes other medical professionals.

The professional organization of occupational therapists is the American Occupational Therapy Association (AOTA). AOTA's *Guidelines for Occupational Therapy Services in School Systems* (originally published in

1989 and currently being updated) outlines the philosophical base of occupational therapy, sets forth standards for practice, states the necessary competencies, describes roles of occupational therapists in schools, and addresses several other issues of school practice.

According to the Bureau of Labor Statistics, in 2001 the mean annual wage of occupational therapists was $52,210. The field is expected to grow faster than the average of all occupations in the first decade of the twenty-first century.

Physical Therapists

Physical therapists are not yet numerous in schools. But like occupational therapy, physical therapy has gained a foothold since the passage of the Education for All Handicapped Children Act and subsequent disability legislation.

In schools the physical therapist has two primary roles. The first, in sports, has a long history. In that role the therapist treats the injuries and the disabilities of athletes. The second role is more general. In this capacity the therapist serves all students. Often at the request of a teacher who recognizes a problem and calls for consultation, the physical therapist evaluates a student and identifies the difficulty. Consultation also is a prominent service of physical therapists in serving students with disabilities under the provisions of the Education for All Handicapped Children Act and subsequent legislation. Physical therapists may provide direct care (hands-on treatment) to students, but more often they help teachers develop a strategy to deal with the diagnosed problem and then monitor progress.

In 2001, there were about 126,450 physical therapists. The Bureau of Labor Statistics projects that employment for physical therapists will grow faster than the average for all occupations through 2010.

To practice, a physical therapist must hold a license in the state in which he or she works. Licensure includes passing a national examination administered by the Professional Examination Service. All physical therapists currently in practice have a license.

Preparation for physical therapy is similar to the premedical curriculum. It includes a strong emphasis on the physical and biological sciences, along with study of psychology and the humanities. Theory and its application are required in a variety of clinical settings. The master's degree or its equivalent now is a minimum requirement for entry into the profession. Master's degree preparation is a six-year program.

According to the Bureau of Labor Statistics, in 2001 the mean annual wage of physical therapists was $59,130.

Speech-Language Pathologists and Audiologists

Speech-language and hearing personnel are closely allied. In 2002, about 118,000 people in the country had training in speech-language pathology and audiology. Almost 90,000 speech-language and hearing specialists held professional certification from the American Speech-Language-Hearing Association (ASHA). Of these, a large portion worked in schools, mostly elementary schools. There are about ten times as many speech-language pathologists as audiologists.

Speech-language pathologists are concerned with evaluation, treatment, and prevention of communication disorders, and with research on the subject. They work with people of all ages, dealing with three types of problems:

1. Speech disorders, including problems with fluency (interrupted flow or rhythm of speech), articulation (difficulty in forming sounds and stringing them together), and voice (inappropriate pitch, quality, loudness, resonance, or duration)
2. Language disorders, including *aphasia* (the loss of speech and language abilities) and delayed language (slowness in developing language skills)
3. *Dysphagia* (difficulty in swallowing)

Speech-language pathologists treat children individually in clinical settings, and they work with teachers in treatment. In some cases they team-teach with teachers.

Since the implementation of the Education for All Handicapped Children Act and subsequent disability legislation, the role of speech-language therapists has changed in a number of ways. They now treat a broader range of children with disabilities, including those who are severely handicapped and those who are multiply handicapped. Treatment begins earlier—down to age three—and greater emphasis is given to speech and language in secondary school programs. Identification and assessment receive greater attention, and more collaboration occurs with teachers, parents, and other school personnel.

Audiologists in schools conduct programs to identify hearing impairment and to prevent such impairment from occurring. They screen and evaluate the hearing of children entering school and provide suggestions, guidance, and counseling to all students. Audiologists consult with teachers, other school personnel, and parents on dealing with hearing and communication problems and on developing IEPs for children with hearing impairments. More specifically, they test children's hearing to determine whether amplification devices are needed, and they recommend the type of device or system that will provide optimal hearing.

Speech-language and hearing personnel are either building based, usually covering two buildings but sometimes more, or itinerant, traveling to a number of schools in a district. A small number practice in district-wide clinics.

ASHA's Certificate of Clinical Competence requires the completion of a master's degree, nine months of supervised professional experience, thirty-six weeks in a postgraduate clinical fellowship, and passing of a national examination. ASHA's standards are more rigorous than state licensure requirements in order to protect the public from incompetent practitioners.

The demand for both speech-language and hearing specialists in schools is healthy. Although demand varies geographically, in general there have been many more jobs than applicants in recent years.

In school systems, speech-language and hearing specialists are on a salary schedule comparable to that for school psychologists and physical and occupational therapists. In school settings in 2002, the median salary for nine- to ten-month contracts was $43,000 for licensed speech-language pathologists, $49,000 for licensed audiologists; and for twelve-month contracts, $51,000 and $54,000, respectively.

FINDING EMPLOYMENT AS A SPECIALIST

Specialists find positions in much the same way that teachers and administrators do—through placement offices in universities (see Chapter 2).

Also, most of them become acquainted with professors in their field while they are engaged in graduate study, and this gives them an advantage over teachers. Professors have contacts with school districts and other employers and often provide leads to their advisees that are more direct and personal than the placement office's standard list of openings.

There also are networks among specialists. They get to know each other in graduate study and through professional association activities. Many leads to employment are communicated through such informal networks.

Some specialists are employed in schools or other agencies on a contract basis. The contract may be with individuals who have the appropriate credentials and training or with an organization, such as a hospital or a clinic in the case of health service personnel. Whatever the arrangement, the professional is usually required to do his or her own marketing of the service to be provided.

FRINGE BENEFITS

The following sections discuss some of the common fringe benefits available to specialists.

Support for Professional Development and Graduate Study

Support for advanced study and training for specialists in school districts or other agencies is much like that provided for school administrative personnel. It depends on whether the specialist is classified as a teacher, a therapist, a consultant, or a supervisor and whether he or she is employed full-time. (Part-time personnel usually do not qualify for fringe benefits.) Benefits and support provided for teachers are described in Chapter 2, and those for personnel in supervisory or administrative categories in Chapters 3 and 4.

Insurance Benefits

Insurance benefits for specialists are as extensive as they are for teachers and administrators. Supervisors' benefits are reported in Chapter 3. Specialists who clearly are teachers may be on a teacher's salary schedule but have slightly better benefits than teachers. Because benefits for specialists often are somewhere between those for teachers and those for administrators, a person interviewing for employment should take special care to learn what he or she will qualify for before signing a contract.

Retirement and Leave Programs

Retirement programs for public school personnel are essentially the same for all levels of professional personnel except some administrators and the superintendent of schools. The program for specialists operates similarly to the programs for teachers, administrators, and supervisors. In health care organizations, programs may be slightly different. Contributions are usually a percentage of salary, so if specialists are paid better, they contribute a greater amount to the program.

Like teachers and other personnel, specialists should be aware that retirement contributions are not transferable across state lines, except in higher education. If a change in employment involves moving to a new state, specialists should inquire whether the contributions of the employer that they are leaving are *vested* (conveyed to the employee as a right) and whether they can buy in to the retirement program of the new state. Vesting locks in the employer's contribution as well as the employee's, and the equity of the annuity so established can stand until retirement if the employee does not withdraw his or her contribution.

Leave provisions for specialists more often are like those for supervisors than those for teachers (see Chapter 3). The specialist is more likely to work an extended school year of ten-and-one-half or eleven months, as administrators and supervisors do.

Opportunities for Outside Employment/Income

Many specialists have something to sell beyond their regular employment. Art and music teachers often give private lessons after school and on Saturdays. If art teachers have time to sketch or paint or sculpt, they can sell their products, provided that the products are good enough. They also can find other alternatives—for example, art therapy, museum work, gallery work, and art for the elderly. Music specialists can play or sing professionally and earn money directing church or civic choirs, the community symphony, or the town band. Physical education specialists can coach after school or in the community in recreation or health centers.

School psychologists report secondary employment in four categories:

1. Independent practice
2. Health and mental health services
3. Business and government
4. Higher education

The opportunities are in counseling, teaching, and consulting. School counselors also have some of these opportunities.

Reading teachers can offer private tutoring sessions, and ESL teachers can find part-time evening employment in adult education or private language centers.

Occupational and physical therapists may engage in private practice or find part-time employment in a clinic or a hospital. Speech-language personnel may provide therapy, and hearing personnel may test people for or consult on hearing problems. Depending on their level of training, all four types of personnel also may teach in adjunct capacities in higher education.

FIRSTHAND ACCOUNT

Chan Evans is an assistant professor at Augusta State University in Georgia. She holds a master's degree in special education from North Carolina State University and is currently working on a doctorate there. Earlier in her career she taught students with emotional and behavioral disorders (EBD) and students with learning disabilities in grades K–8. She recalls how she got started, talks about upsides and downsides, and offers advice.

Before becoming a special educator, I taught horseback riding. One of my students was a professor in special education, and I became interested in the field through conversations with her about working with students with learning disabilities and reading problems. When I decided to change careers, my initial plan was to work for a few years as a teacher's assistant at a public separate school for adolescents with severe behavior disorders while I completed a master's degree in reading. However, because of the tremendous shortage of special educators in general, and of EBD specialists in particular, my teaching career began after only two months as a teacher's assistant.

That year was one of the most challenging and difficult of my life. I taught a self-contained class of ninth-grade males with EBD and quickly realized that I was ill-prepared to perform many of the requisite tasks. I was responsible for teaching all the courses in the ninth-grade curriculum, and that in itself was daunting. I struggled with lesson planning, behavior management, special education paperwork, school committees, and a general lack of support from the administration, regular educators, and parents.

There were enough inspiring moments and connections with students to see me through, but by the spring I knew that the only way I could continue in the field was to go back to school full-time and learn how to do all the things that were expected in the job.

The year as a master's degree student was incredibly valuable. I returned to public school with a renewed enthusiasm for working with youngsters with challenging behaviors and academic deficits.

Upsides and Downsides
General education teachers used to tell me repeatedly that they could *never* work with the population of students I chose to teach. Yes, there were downsides to working with students whose behaviors and emotions are so different, intense, or disturbing that their educational performance is affected enough to warrant separate individualized special education services. Many of them, especially the older ones, are incorrigible. I eventually chose to work with younger students because of my desire to see a relationship between my efforts and an increase in prosocial behaviors.

There are settings in special education besides the self-contained classroom, but I preferred it. Although planning and teaching several levels simultaneously was quite challenging, I liked having students of different ages and abilities within the same class. After I acquired the necessary skills, I also enjoyed some of the very characteristics of the job that made the first year so difficult. What I at first saw as isolation I later learned to appreciate as autonomy. I was free to instigate almost any program I could justify as being both educational and engaging. Over the years my students were involved in gardening projects, were peer helpers for students with severe physical and cognitive disabilities, and studied academics using a horse theme, complete with six weeks of horseback riding lessons.

The amount of paperwork necessary in special education is notoriously burdensome, partly because each student has an individualized education program (IEP) that must be assessed and updated regularly. The class size is much smaller than in general education, but there are additional responsibilities, including attending multidisciplinary team meetings, compliance meetings, and parent meetings; making modifications to instruction and testing; and creating and assessing behavioral intervention and support plans.

Advice

The good news is that you always can get a job teaching students with disabilities. The bad news is that you may not last long if you don't learn quickly how to revel in small successes, enjoy your students, and teach them worthwhile skills. Also, it is essential to have a supportive administration. Before you accept a job, ask the principal to explain his or her philosophy about students with disabilities and his or her views about inclusion. Look for evidence of integration and support. It is important to connect with other educators in your school and community. Ask for assistance and offer your talents. Learn to collaborate with co-workers and parents. Keep yourself fresh and your skills current by becoming knowledgeable in other areas of special education. Most certificates allow you to teach K–12, so consider changing settings or age groups when you feel burnout creeping in. Stay connected with your university classmates, and continue to read professional journals. Get involved with the Council for Exceptional Children, and consider presenting at a conference. Know that you are doing important and difficult work, and pace yourself accordingly.

CHAPTER

6

TEACHING, RESEARCH, AND ADMINISTRATION IN HIGHER EDUCATION

There are romantic notions of higher education that come partly from the nostalgic recollections of those who have experienced it and partly from Hollywood depictions of college life. Walls with dangling ivy, heroics on the football field, fraternity and sorority parties, and unending opportunities for students to find mates are part of those sweet-and-easy views. Probably all of these conditions and events can be found on college campuses, but they are peripherals, not the main focus.

Academe actually is much like a business. Students are interested in credits, grades, and degrees. They see college as the key path to satisfying jobs and good salaries—the better the performance in college, the better the job possibilities. Anyone who visits a higher education institution will quickly see that assessment and accountability are the major concerns of students, faculty, and administrators.

Yet a visitor would notice other important trends, among them:

- New strategies being initiated to improve access and educational success for diverse students
- Rising costs due to decreasing support of universities and community colleges by state legislatures
- An evolving understanding of the college student as a learner
- An increasing focus on assessment of performance outcomes for students and institutions

- Creation of dynamic learning experiences for students through greater use of inquiry-based teaching and technology-enabled tools
- Expanding responsibilities for faculty and administrators, including larger classes, broadening expectations to use nontraditional systems of delivering instruction, increasing workloads, and reaffirmation of a responsibility for student civic engagement and service learning

Teaching, research, and administrative careers in higher education are numerous and diverse. Table 6.1 presents a historical picture of higher education's dramatic growth since 1870, a year in which only one doctor's degree and no master's degrees were awarded. The total annual expenditure for higher education now exceeds $190 billion. More than 1 million faculty and instructional staff teach almost 14.8 million students in nearly 4,000 colleges and universities. These figures include all public and private two- and four-year institutions of higher education. Almost one-half million students earned degrees in graduate and professional schools in 2000.

During the 1970s, college enrollment was relatively stable. In the 1980s it increased more than 30 percent. From the late 1980s to the early 1990s, there was a 12 percent increase. Further, there were steady increases during the 1990s.

The typical age of college students has been eighteen to twenty-four years. However, in the last twenty years, the age makeup of undergraduates has changed. No longer do nearly all students come to college directly from high school. In 1999, 58 percent of students were eighteen to twenty-four years of age, and 42 percent were twenty-five years of age or older.

The percentages of women and minority students also have increased. Since 1986, women have accounted for more than half the total enrollment in institutions of higher education. Since 1982, they have earned more than half of the bachelor's degrees, and since 1985, more than half of the master's degrees. In 1999, women represented 56 percent of the total college enrollment. In 1976, 16 percent of American college students were minorities, compared with 28 percent in 1999. Asian and Hispanic students have made up the majority of increases in minority enrollment. The percentage of African-American students increased from 9.6 percent in 1976 to 11.6 percent in 1999.

Educators in two- and four-year colleges and universities teach and administer in hundreds of disciplines and fields. In four-year colleges and universities, they also do research. Some higher education faculty teach exclusively; this is most true in two-year colleges, where a large portion of personnel work part-time. However, in two-year colleges most of the full-time faculty *teach* full-time.

Research is conducted in universities, where faculty typically spend half of their time teaching and at least a third of their time doing research. Teaching is by far the primary function in four-year and comprehensive colleges. Some four-year college faculty and many university professors also do descriptive or empirical research, which entails laboratory work or field-

Table 6.1 Growth in Higher Education, 1870–2000

Year	Number of States	U.S. Population	Number of Institutions[1]	Faculty	Enrollment	Earned Degrees Conferred			Total Expenditure (in thousands)
						Bachelor's[2]	Master's[3]	Doctor's	
1869–1870	37	38,558,371	563	5,553	52,286	9,371	0	1	ND
1879–1880	38	50,189,209	811	11,522	115,817	12,896	879	54	ND
1889–1890	44	62,979,766	998	15,809	156,756	15,539	1,015	149	ND
1899–1900	45	76,212,168	977	23,868	237,592	27,410	1,583	382	ND
1909–1910	46	92,228,496	951	36,480	355,213	37,199	2,113	443	ND
1919–1920	48	106,021,537	1,041	48,615	597,880	48,622	4,279	615	ND
1929–1930	48	123,202,624	1,409	82,386	1,100,737	122,484	14,969	2,299	507,142
1939–1940	48	132,164,569	1,708	146,929	1,494,203	186,500	26,731	3,290	674,688
1949–1950	48	151,325,798	1,851	246,722	2,659,021	432,058	58,183	6,420	2,245,661
1959–1960	50	179,323,175	2,008	380,554	3,215,544	392,440	74,435	9,829	5,601,376
1969–1970	50	203,302,031	2,525	450,000	7,136,075	792,656	208,291	29,866	21,043,113
1979–1980	50	226,542,580	3,152	675,000	11,569,899	929,417	298,081	32,615	56,913,588
1989–1990	50	249,400,000	3,535	824,220	13,538,560	1,051,344	324,301	38,371	134,655,571
1999–2000	50	288,358,511	3,958	1,134,163	14,791,224	1,193,000[4]	440,000[4]	47,100[4]	190,476,162

ND = No data
[1] Before 1980, excludes branch campuses.
[2] From 1870 to 1960, includes first-professional degrees.
[3] Master's except first-professional degrees; beginning in 1970, includes all master's degrees.
[4] Projected figure.

Sources: From *Digest of Education Statistics 1995* (p. 175), by T. D. Snyder, 1995, Washington, DC: National Center for Education Statistics; *Projections of Education Statistics to 2011* (30th ed.), by D. E. Gerald and W. J. Hussar, 2001, Washington, DC: National Center for Education Statistics; *National Study of Postsecondary Faculty, Institutional Survey*, 1999, 2001, Washington, DC: National Center for Education Statistics; and *The Chronicle of Higher Education Almanac*, 2000, Washington, DC: The Chronicle of Higher Education.

work, reviews of the literature, and searches of other databases. With publishing as a requirement for promotion, many four-year college and university faculty members write scholarly or scientific articles and books. Those in the humanities may write plays, novels, or poetry. Senior faculty often administer a department while continuing to teach. Many university professors have five responsibilities: teaching, program design and assessment, research, writing, and service. Administrative responsibilities often constitute a sixth responsibility.

Many of the points made in Chapter 2 about teaching as an art and a science apply to college teaching as well as K–12 teaching. Readers may want to read those parts of Chapter 2 in conjunction with this chapter in order to get a fuller picture of the generic nature of teaching.

A 1999 publication, *Higher Education Trends for the Next Century*, highlights trends that are effecting changes in the higher education workplace: technology, financial hardship, more clearly focused mission statements, new forms of accountability and assessment, changing student characteristics, and a renewed commitment to student learning and development. Student affairs professionals, for example, now are engaging in more deliberate attempts to measure the effects of their work on student outcomes—such as persistence, learning, intellectual and moral development, satisfaction, and commitment to citizenship. Student affairs professionals also are examining the effects of various technological applications on services to students.

FOUR-YEAR COLLEGES AND UNIVERSITIES

Educators in four-year colleges and universities typically engage in teaching and research, or administration.

Teaching and Research in Four-Year Colleges and Universities

The college context strongly influences teaching in four-year colleges and universities. For example, college professors do not have to deal with discipline. College is voluntary. Students generally come expecting to conform reasonably to the protocols of college life, whatever these might entail at a particular institution. Nonetheless, like K–12 teaching, college teaching varies greatly in terms of the professor's beliefs about learning, the nature of the subject matter taught, the role of the institution in educating students, and the function of the teacher.

College teaching is shaped, at least in part, by the characteristics, the policies, and the practices of the employing institution. Higher education, as already indicated, takes place in large, middle-sized, and small institutions. Most students attend large universities, many of which are urban. The combination of a large institution and an urban setting makes it difficult for students to get acquainted with their classmates and nearly impossible for professors to know their students. Classes of 300 to 500, conducted in an auditorium, are common, particularly for first- and second-year students.

The same universities that have such large classes also offer advanced undergraduate courses and graduate seminars that are much smaller in size. Sometimes they include only a handful of students. The professor in these settings has close contact with each student and probably knows many of them well. Because by this time the students have chosen a major and many of them already are specializing within it, the professor perhaps has had interactions with them in several prior courses and in other activities. Evaluation of learning often is informal and is related to actual performance, laboratory work, empirical or theoretical research, and papers prepared by the student. There is give-and-take, criticism, and feedback. The professor often serves in the role of mentor and may be the major adviser to one or two of the seminar members. A professor teaching a large class usually also teaches one of these small classes. In addition, he or she participates in committees, advises students, conducts research, and writes. All these activities constitute that professor's faculty load.

At smaller undergraduate residential colleges, a professor may teach three or four courses per semester, maintain office hours to consult with advisees and students from his or her classes, and serve on department or college committees. Each course may be a combination of lecture and discussion. Student learning is evaluated in a variety of ways. Students prepare papers (often including a term paper), take essay-type examinations, participate in class discussions, and have individual conferences with the professor. To assess the students' abilities and knowledge, the professor reads and grades written assignments, interviews individuals, coaches them, and critiques their work.

Professors in state colleges, often those at the assistant and associate rank, may teach four courses and often more than one section of the same course. This is considered a full undergraduate teaching load. They may lecture most of the time because it enables them to cover the syllabus and because preparation of lectures is so time consuming that planning greater diversity in method is impossible. Learning is evaluated by means of frequent examination and assigned papers. Personal conferences occur when initiated by the student or the professor. Classes and office hours are scheduled during the daytime. In addition to teaching, these professors are assigned a number of advisees; the relationship with advisees often involves approving course loads at registration time. The college is committed primarily to teaching, but administrators notice those who have contributed to important journals when promotions are considered.

Preparation

Professors and administrators in colleges and universities typically have earned bachelor's, master's, and doctor's degrees. Some have skipped the middle degree and continued without interruption from the bachelor's to the doctor's degree. A doctor's degree is essential if one expects to proceed up the career ladder in four-year colleges and universities. In two-year colleges a master's degree often is adequate. (The two-year college is characterized by a different career system, which is described later in this chapter.)

Selecting the institutions at which one prepares for a career in higher education can be very important. Anyone who aspires early in life to an academic career would be wise to select carefully a college for undergraduate study. If the information is obtainable, one should choose a college for its reputation in one's chosen field of study and for the reputations of professors in that field. Often, faculty recommend students for admission and fellowships. In universities, professors encourage their most able students to undertake graduate study. In graduate school, selecting a major adviser who is prominent in one's field is central to receiving good guidance and often is an important link to initial employment and advancement in the field after graduation.

In the course of graduate study, there is time and opportunity to survey job possibilities. Making decisions about the type and the size of institution that fit one's career aspirations requires considerable thought and probably some compromise. Not infrequently, prospective professors seek to teach and do research in an institution exactly like the one at which they earned their doctorate. Some important questions a prospective professor should ask are: Is my major interest teaching? Am I more inclined toward research? Which institutions have the strongest faculties? Which have adequate access to library and other resources?

The job market, of course, determines how much choice the prospective college teacher or researcher has. Irrespective of the job market, however, the selection of an institution for employment is important to the candidate and to the institution. Place of employment is a major factor in a young professor's quality of life, and it often determines the extent of support and encouragement that will be forthcoming from the administration. Students of higher education use the term *fit* to describe the compatibility of a candidate and an institution. Fit has social, intellectual, and cultural dimensions. It includes lifestyle, philosophical (and sometimes religious) persuasion, social class, devotion to intellectual pursuits, and cosmopolitanism. Fit also may have snobbish manifestations. Higher education is not immune to esoteric stodginess and stubborn tradition. A new faculty member, although freshly charged with ideas for reform and renewal, may make little difference if his or her ideas diverge too far from those of the entrenched professors. Neophytes hardly ever reform an establishment, and trying to do so is usually more punishing to them than to veterans.

Career Patterns

On completion of the doctor's degree, a person's first college or university position is usually an assistant professorship, though it may be an instructorship. Assistant professors may be hired on a *tenure track*—that is, a course that puts them in line for promotion to permanent employment— or in a temporary position with no assurance of a job after the term of the appointment. Prospective faculty should be aware that being hired on a temporary appointment often results in their jumping from job to job, and the more movement they make of this type, the more difficult it may become to find tenured employment anywhere.

The probationary period for an instructor or an assistant professor usually lasts a number of years. Typically, a new faculty member will submit a professional vita for reappointment after three years in a particular institution of higher education. Such a vita consists of evidence of his or her accomplishments: publications, research reports, papers presented at professional meetings, college achievements, activities in professional associations and learned societies, and anything else that attests to fulfillment of institutional goals and objectives. Both the application and the evidence are packaged and submitted according to guidelines established by the college or university.

After review of the vita by department and college faculty, the faculty member usually is reappointed. At the beginning of the sixth year, the faculty member submits another professional vita, for review for promotion and tenure. Typically, this vita is reviewed by the department faculty, a college personnel committee, the college dean, the university personnel committee, and the president or chancellor. At any step in this sequence, a decision can be made to deny or recommend promotion with tenure.

The American Association of University Professors (AAUP) recommends that "notice . . . be given at least one year prior to the expiration of the probationary period if the teacher is not to be continued in service after the expiration of that period." If tenure is not granted, the individual has no future at the institution, and "the appointment for the following year becomes a terminal one."

The success or the failure of a professor at a particular institution may not be strictly a matter of competence. Success may occur because of congruity with the criteria mentioned earlier, or failure may result because of conflict with one of them. Young professors should recognize that they may be successful in one context and not in another.

The professor earns greater status as he or she moves up the academic ladder. Promotion usually also means opportunities to teach more specialized courses and upper-division or graduate students. The institution allows more time for research and writing, particularly at the university level, and it places greater importance on such activity.

The professor actually operates in two realms: that of the employing institution and that of his or her chosen discipline. The latter often commands the greater loyalty and holds the primary interest. As a result, it is not unusual for professors to build more networks with colleagues at other institutions who are in their field than with colleagues at their own institution who are not in their field.

With promotion, however, their contacts with professors in other fields at their own institution increase. Greater participation in setting policy at the department, college, and institution level is a responsibility of promotion in rank.

Promotion to full professor, which for most people comes after a number of additional years of satisfactory service, increases responsibilities and privileges. The broader institutional concerns that professors develop in all-college committee work sometimes provide the motivation to move into higher education administration.

Professors who spend most or all of their time in research are a somewhat special breed. They often begin a commitment to research while they are studying for an advanced degree. They earn a doctorate and become involved with a *mentor*, or major professor, in research activity. Research for the doctoral dissertation often is a segment of a larger study being directed by the mentor. Although many Ph.D. candidates take this route to meeting requirements, only a few continue with a major or full career commitment to research. Support for research professors in academe exists almost exclusively in the leading universities and institutes, and most of that support comes from outside funding by government, business, and industry. The typical research professor's responsibility therefore consists, in part, of seeking contracts and grants for further study. Not infrequently, a professor's research is shaped by the availability of funds for specified projects. In fact, there is considerable criticism in academic circles that too much influence on the direction and the nature of research comes from outside the university.

There are many career paths, including some fairly common career changes. Some of the options for career changes that academics take are discussed later in this chapter.

The particulars of teaching or research careers in the arts and sciences and in the many professional fields are not explored here. That subject would call for a book in itself. Three main sources provide specific information on core undergraduate teaching fields, graduate study, and professional and specialized graduate schools. In the first two categories (undergraduate and graduate education) are the American Council of Learned Societies and the associations that represent the various disciplines, such as the American Anthropological Association and the American Institute of Biological Sciences. For professional and specialized graduate schools, the corresponding associations (for example, the American Bar Association, the American Medical Association, and the American Institute of Architects) and the respective accrediting agencies provide information on admission requirements, application procedures, academic expectations, internships or other requirements for practical experience, career opportunities and demand, accredited schools, cost of preparation, projected salaries, and scholarships and fellowships.

Administration in Four-Year Colleges and Universities

Administration in the college or university is a very different responsibility than it is in K–12 schools. The size, purpose, commitment, affiliation, reputation, and source of financial support of an institution are among the factors that influence what administrators the institution employs and what those administrators do. Also, national trends and new federal policies shape the work of higher education administrators.

Within the ranks of administration, there are a variety of different positions, but five general groupings are recognized: executive, academic, administrative, student affairs, and external affairs. Table 6.2 lists about 100 major positions typically found in each grouping in two- and four-year colleges and universities, public and private. No institution has all the jobs listed in Table 6.2. Small institutions may combine some of them, and large institutions may split some.

Many more positions exist that are subordinate to those named in Table 6.2—for example, associate and assistant deans. Also, the list does not include the administrators of the individual units that make up a college or professional school, such as heads of departments or divisions.

The number of positions and their configuration vary primarily by size. The larger an institution is, the more positions it will have, including separate ones for such functions as development and public relations. Slight variation also exists by control of institution, most notably the presence of a position for director of church relations at private institutions.

Academic administration is basic to the institution and has the longest history. As a result, it is the most prestigious. Its practitioners emerge from the disciplines, from the ranks of professors. Indeed, department heads are usually elected or appointed from among the professors in a department; sometimes they are hired from outside the institution. Other academic administrators often come from outside the institution, attracted by a regional or national search.

Many academic administrators, particularly department heads, teach as well as administer. Deans and their associates and assistants may or may not teach. However, some institutions take great pride in keeping academic administrators involved in teaching. The practice helps them stay in touch

Table 6.2 Administrative Positions in Two- and Four-Year Colleges and Universities, by Job Families

	Two-Year College	Four-Year College	University
Executive Positions			
Chief executive officer, system (chancellor)			X
Chief executive officer, single institution (president)	X	X	X
Assistant to chief executive officer, single institution	X	X	X
Academic Positions			
Chief academic officer (provost)			X
Chief health-professions officer	X	X	X
Director, library services	X	X	X
Acquisitions librarian	X	X	X
Chief technical services librarian	X	X	X
Chief public services librarian	X	X	X
Reference librarian	X	X	X
Catalog librarian	X	X	X
Director, institutional research	X	X	X
Director, educational media services center	X	X	X
Director, international education	X	X	X
Director, academic computing	X	X	X
Director, sponsored research and programs	X	X	X
Deans			
Agriculture	X		X
Architecture			X
Arts and sciences	X	X	X
Business	X	X	X
Communications	X	X	X
Continuing education	X	X	X
Dentistry			X
Education	X	X	X
Engineering	X	X	X
Extension	X		X
Fine arts	X	X	X
Graduate programs		X	X
Health-related professions	X	X	X

continued

Table 6.2, *continued* Administrative Positions in Two- and Four-Year Colleges and Universities, by Job Families

	Two-Year College	Four-Year College	University
Humanities	x	x	x
Instruction	x		
Law	x	x	x
Library and information sciences	x	x	x
Medicine			x
Music		x	x
Nursing	x	x	x
Occupational and vocational education	x	x	x
Pharmacy			x
Public health			x
Social sciences	x	x	x
Social work		x	x
Veterinary medicine			x
Administrative Positions			
Chief business or financial officer	x	x	x
Chief administrative officer	x	x	x
Director, environmental health and safety	x	x	x
Director, telecommunications and networking	x	x	x
Chief planning officer	x	x	x
Chief budget officer	x	x	x
General counsel	x	x	x
Staff attorney		x	x
Chief human resources officer	x	x	x
Manager, employee relations and benefits	x	x	x
Manager, training and development	x	x	x
Director, affirmative action and equal employment opportunity	x	x	x
Chief information systems officer	x	x	x
Database administrator	x	x	x
Systems analyst	x	x	x
Programmer analyst	x	x	x
Director, administrative computing	x	x	x
Chief physical plant officer	x	x	x

Table 6.2, *continued* Administrative Positions in Two- and Four-Year Colleges
and Universities, by Job Families

	Two-Year College	Four-Year College	University
Associate director, physical plant	x	x	x
Manager, landscape and grounds	x	x	x
Manager, custodial services	x	x	x
Manager, power plant	x	x	x
Comptroller	x	x	x
Manager, payroll	x	x	x
Director, accounting	x	x	x
Bursar	x	x	x
Director, purchasing	x	x	x
Director, bookstore	x	x	x
Director, internal audit	x	x	x
Director, auxiliary services	x	x	x
Manager, mail services	x	x	x
Director, campus security	x	x	x
Administrator, hospital medical center			x
Director, medical center public relations			x
Director, medical center personnel			x
Student Services Positions			
Student affairs officer	x	x	x
Dean of students	x	x	x
Registrar	x	x	x
Director, admissions and student financial aid	x	x	x
Director, food services	x	x	x
Director, student housing	x	x	x
Director, student union and student activities	x	x	x
Director, foreign students	x	x	x
Director, career development and placement	x	x	x
Director, student counseling	x	x	x
Associate director, counseling	x	x	x
Director, student health services		x	x
Director, athletics	x	x	x
Director, men's athletics	x	x	x
Director, women's athletics	x	x	x

continued

Table 6.2, *continued* Administrative Positions in Two- and Four-Year Colleges
and Universities, by Job Families

	Two-Year College	Four-Year College	University
Director, sports information	X	X	X
Director, campus recreation	X	X	X
Director, minority affairs	X	X	X
External Affairs Positions			
Chief development officer	X	X	X
Director, annual giving	X	X	X
Director, corporate and foundation relations	X	X	X
Director, planned giving	X	X	X
Chief public relations officer	X	X	X
Director, governmental relations	X	X	X
Director, alumni affairs	X	X	X
Director, community services	X	X	X
Director, publications	X	X	X
Manager, printing services	X	X	X
Director, information office	X	X	X

Source: Adapted from "Fact File: Median Salaries of College Administrators by Type
of Institution, 1996–97," *Chronicle of Higher Education*, February 21, 1997.

with their field and with students. Also, it reduces the guilt that many
feel about leaving their field by enabling them to maintain a partial tie,
and it keeps the road back to teaching open. The latter is practical as well
as idealistic because the work of administration in most cases is not akin
to the work of an academic discipline. In administration, former professors may lose contact with their discipline and colleagues, and the loss
often is irreversible. Moreover, among academics there is a measure of dis-
dain for administrators, even though most administrators are former
professors.

Executive administration is a modern phenomenon, a product of the
enormous growth of the academic enterprise in the twentieth century. In
earlier times, when all institutions of higher education had relatively small
enrollments, the president of an institution was at least a former professor,

if not an active one, and had academic responsibilities. That is still true in small colleges. But in large colleges and universities, although most presidents were once academics, they now are exclusively top-level managers with no academic responsibilities.

The job of executive or academic administrator does have some special requirements. Deans, provosts, presidents, and *chancellors* (used here to refer to the chief executive officers of entire systems of higher education institutions) must rise above their discipline. They must be concerned with institutional goals and achievements (one reason that former colleagues see them as lost to the discipline). Their breadth of responsibility and their place in the hierarchy determine the scope of perspective necessary. All must have a broad knowledge of higher education, including the capacity to view the relative importance of current events and trends, and a vision of direction for the future. They must have a notion of appropriate mission and be aware of how their institution ranks among and relates to comparable ones in the country. Skills in gaining support and understanding from outside groups are essential to finding resources for operating a dynamic institution. Such groups include state boards of education, state legislators, members of the college or university's board of trustees, philanthropic foundations, alumni, and the various communications media.

Academic administrators deal with the mission of their department, school, or university; curriculum content and courses; standards for selection and retention of students; and interpretation, application, and creation of policies relating to academic matters. They manage recruitment, hiring, evaluation, promotion, and dismissal of faculty. Schedules, space allocation, and budget also are in their province. They promote research and facilitate support of it. Department heads represent their faculty members at college-wide meetings and to their dean, and deans are the link to the university's top academic administrator.

Administrative, external affairs, and student affairs positions are other important examples of administrative roles. They are more recent additions to higher education administration functions that were separated out as institutions became larger and as the role of higher education became more complex.

Nonacademic administrators and executives, in a sense, relieve academic administrators of many details, most responsibilities for external and student affairs, and a large portion of the relationships with governing boards (in the case of state-supported institutions, with statewide boards, special commissions, legislators, and the executive branch). Where once an academic administrator managed all the tasks, in larger institutions the tasks now are distributed across several domains. Academic responsibilities remain with the academic administrators, but many of the other chores are assumed by nonacademic administrators or executives.

Perhaps the primary roles of the chief executive officer are fund-raiser and policy maker. He or she seeks to enlarge the institution's endowments. An institution's vitality often is associated with the size of its endowment. As well, he or she must see the big picture of the nation and the world that the institution serves and in which it functions. Advice and opinion on policy come from faculty senates and deans and vice presidents, but the head person must make the decisions.

The chief executive officer has additional duties. For example, the national and international interests and responsibilities of the university typically flow from, or are nurtured by, the chief executive officer's desk. Legal matters, institutional funding, and relationships with people in the state, the region, and the nation—all fall to the top officer. The president of a single institution or the chancellor of a system makes the final decisions and is the public spokesperson.

Although five categories of administration are identified in Table 6.2, the executive, administrative, and external affairs functions are so close in many institutions that they are organized together and managed by the executive officer.

A function that typically stands alone is the business operation, which handles tuition, endowments, taxes, grants, contracts, purchasing, payroll, and sundry other matters. Business personnel, often managed by a chief officer at the level of vice president, may not come from the ranks of academe. Their training often is in such areas as accounting, marketing, management, and finance.

Public relations is increasingly important to colleges and universities. The people who communicate to the public and the media on behalf of the institution often are trained in public affairs, journalism, or communications. In institutions with a radio or television station, the staff are media-trained people—that is, they are professionals in their field, not usually academics.

Student affairs administrators, such as the dean of students, the dean of men, and the dean of women, often do not come up through academic ranks. Rather, they are trained as specialists in guidance and student personnel work, dealing with such aspects of college and university life as housing, fraternities and sororities, service learning, student leadership and governance, and student activities (events and organizations). The domain of student affairs officers often overlaps with that of academic administrators—for example, in scholarships, loans, eligibility, suspensions, re-admissions, and expulsions.

Student affairs professionals have begun to reconceptualize their role in student life and learning. They argue that student learning and development occur both in and outside the college classroom. As well, they are encouraging more holistic views of student learning and student abilities. For example, they propose that critical thinking and relating to others be integrated in higher education programs. Student affairs professionals also propose that higher education nurture civic responsibility and productive citizenship through extracurricular or cocurricular experiences.

Preparation

Large universities offer graduate degree programs in higher education administration and student affairs. These programs typically include courses and internships.

However, some academic administrators come up through the ranks and learn most of their knowledge and skills on the job.

The position of department head is usually filled by a professor elected to the post. In many cases the position rotates among the full professors in a department. The next step, to assistant or associate dean, may come as a result of a dean's encouragement to a professor to apply, but selection almost always is from a pool of candidates who actually apply for an opening when it is advertised. Experience as a department head or other middle-level manager in a college or university is good background for an assistant or associate deanship. In fact, it is important in a résumé when applying for any college-wide administrative post.

Training for top positions in universities is almost nonexistent. Some people holding them are academics; others are businesspeople, professionals, military officers, or politicians. Their common characteristic is administrative experience. But here too, many have not studied or taken a degree in higher education administration. Business, student affairs, and external affairs officers also may not be academics and may come from a variety of backgrounds.

Career Patterns

A number of professors try administration, and many stay with it, although some return to teaching and research. When motivated, they may by chance or through initiative move up some or all of the steps in the administrative ladder from department head, to assistant or associate dean, to dean, and on to provost, vice president, president, and chancellor. The promotion they desire is often not available at their institution of current employment. In such instances they must find an appropriate position at another institution. However, experience in more than one college or university broadens perspective and enlarges the contacts and the reputation of an administrator.

Tracking the careers of administrators in higher education reveals some patterns. For example, administrators in private colleges and universities tend to remain in their type of institution, and administrators in public institutions in theirs.

Finding Employment

Teaching and administrative positions are usually advertised, and consideration is given to all candidates who apply. Other things being equal, however, two factors prove to be influential in a candidate's gaining an edge:

1. A track record and a reputation that are personally known by the people at the employing institution who are screening applicants
2. Ties to those same people through work in professional associations

Obviously, then, the knowledge that professors and administrators develop of one another over time in work and extra-institutional relationships often carries weight in who gets a job. As a consequence, specific advice on how to find employment is difficult to provide.

When a candidate maintains connections with his or her graduate school, he or she can be alerted to openings by the placement office. Advertisements of openings appear in the *Chronicle of Higher Education*, the *New York Times*, and professional journals. Personal networks always are at work in bringing news of openings. There is no prescription for getting from knowing of an available position to being one of the few under consideration. But a candidate who has had an opportunity to demonstrate abilities to the people who will be asked to make recommendations will certainly have a distinct advantage over the other applicants.

Positions as deans, provosts, presidents, and chancellors are widely advertised in newspapers and journals. The *Chronicle of Higher Education* and the *New York Times* regularly carry advertisements of open positions. Professional searchers work on contract with boards of regents and other governing bodies to find and screen candidates. Candidates may come from any place in the country. Preliminary screening may be done on the basis of credentials, résumés, telephone inquiries, and letters outlining experience, training, and interest. A committee typically conducts the search and identifies three to five candidates who best meet the standards it has set (which are usually advertised). Finalists are invited to the campus for interviews, and preferences are recommended to the appropriate officer or, in the case of president or chancellor, to the appropriate board. In most cases, decisions to hire at the dean's level and above must be approved by the governing board.

Administrative jobs, particularly top positions, have been rather short stints in recent years. Hence, in initial contract negotiations, successful candidates have sought provisions to protect themselves in the event of premature or unexpected termination. For example, a candidate for a deanship may seek a concurrent appointment as a full professor with tenure; then if he or she resigns or is deposed, some job security remains. Another provision for protection may be severance pay. Some provisions are sufficiently desirable to be labeled "golden parachutes."

Related Careers

Despite Seymour Sarason's pronouncement (in *You Are Thinking of Teaching?*) that academics is a "one life–one career" profession, opportunities for employment outside academe evolve from being a professor or an administrator in higher education. They depend on one's specialty, however. For example, a professor of economics or geology may readily find employment in government or business, whereas a professor of classics seldom is called on to work in other than an academic setting.

Many professors and administrators are appointed to state and federal government positions, which they occupy for part or all of a particular administration or for some other period. Employment outside the university may offer respite from academe and an opportunity to apply knowledge in the "real world." Some who take such appointments eventually return to an academic post, but others find a new career. For example, Paul Wellstone was a professor before becoming a U.S. senator. Daniel Patrick Moynihan was a former professor who spent considerable time in government. Further, Donna Shalala served as a university president before joining President Bill Clinton's cabinet, and Condoleezza Rice, Stanford University's first African-American provost, became the national security adviser in the administration of George W. Bush.

University policy usually limits the time a professor can take leave for outside service. When that period is up, the choice is to return or to resign.

Outside Employment

Employment outside the institution is usually part-time and is in addition to work for the institution and a regular teaching load. It takes place during full-time employment, not during a leave of absence. Many professors seek opportunities in their field to teach an extra course, to be a guest professor on a neighboring campus, or to consult outside the university in their specialty. In some institutions, extra employment becomes so time consuming that restrictions are imposed on the amount of time that professors may spend in it.

In such fields as engineering, economics, political science, business administration, geology, education, and health services, professors can find operational systems that apply their discipline. They can try new ideas and test experimental constructs, assist people in improving performance, and engage their students in the real world of practice.

Salary and Fringe Benefits

Salary does not seem to be the major incentive among higher education faculty and administrators that it is in other walks of life. For example, conditions that are as important as salary in attracting and holding professors are administrative support, teaching loads, research budgets and assistants, library and laboratory facilities, and stimulating colleagues. In *Publication, Teaching, and the Academic Reward Structure*, Howard Tuckman says, "In college teaching, salary is not the measure of power, prestige, and success; other factors often substitute for salary in a person's decision to move or remain at an institution."

Salary, on the other hand, is not unimportant. Salaries vary, by rank, by control and type of institution, and by discipline. Table 6.3 presents data on some of these variables for professors. Table 6.4 offers figures for selected administrative positions.

Incentives and rewards for college and university faculty are more than monetary. Many are not counted and reported in aggregate. Privileges and resources such as library holdings, laboratory facilities, computer capacity, research and teaching assistants, and secretarial help are not surveyed and

Table 6.3 Average Salaries (in Dollars) of Four-Year College and University Professors by Type of Institution, Control of Institution, and Rank, 2000–01

	Assistant Professor	Associate Professor	Professor
Doctoral-Level Institutions			
Public	53,392	63,049	89,631
Private independent	64,149	73,470	112,534
Private church-related	56,863	68,045	89,426
Comprehensive Institutions			
Public	47,476	57,780	72,770
Private independent	48,501	59,442	77,130
Private church-related	46,218	56,774	73,328
General Baccalaureate Institutions			
Public	43,789	54,451	64,508
Private independent	45,368	54,929	76,692
Private church-related	40,575	48,186	58,927

Source: From *Quite Good News—for Now: The Annual Report of the Economic State of the Profession*, by American Association of University Professors, 2002, Washington, DC: Author.

Table 6.4 Median Salaries (in Dollars) of Selected University and Four-Year
College Administrators, 2001–02

	University	Four-Year College
Chief executive officer	267,148	NA
Chief academic officer	183,297	88,294
Director, library services	118,168	58,900
Director, academic computing	94,000	62,109
Dean, arts and sciences	146,932	67,000
Dean, business	175,208	71,984
Dean, education	130,858	69,517
Dean, engineering	170,642	89,328
Dean, fine arts	134,160	63,277
Dean, graduate programs	124,292	75,000
Dean, law	202,400	NA
Dean, music	125,000	52,225
Chief business officer	158,000	100,132
Chief financial officer	140,000	78,200
Chief personnel/human resources officer	102,610	58,250
Director, administrative computing	99,037	63,792
Chief development officer	147,335	95,507
Director, corporate and foundation relations	78,110	55,000
Chief public relations officer	111,806	58,120
Director, governmental relations	102,480	59,019
Chief student affairs officer	137,125	82,359
Chief admissions officer	84,242	64,913
Registrar	79,563	50,735
Director, food services	81,637	60,648
Director, student housing	75,195	41,700
Director, student activities	66,482	43,438
Director, student health services, physician	112,165	98,615
Director, athletics	132,301	62,936

Source: Adapted from "Facts & Figures: Median Salaries of College Administrators
by Type of Institution, 2001–2002," *Chronicle of Higher Education*, April 12, 2002.

reported as benefits. Perhaps they are central rather than fringe. Nevertheless, they should be assessed in seeking employment because their availability or absence fosters or detracts from effective functioning.

AAUP and the National Center for Education Statistics collect information and report on the welfare of professors. Their data include salary, fringe benefits, and tenure. Tenure is a benefit, although often not reported as such, and it is an elusive benefit for some. About 64 percent of full-time faculty had tenure in 1998–99, but a large gender difference existed: 71 percent of men had tenure, compared with 52 percent of women. Obviously, women need to be more inquiring about tenure practices than men, preferably before employment.

AAUP reports monetary rewards in two categories: salary and compensation. Compensation is higher than salary because it includes fringe benefits. Fringe benefits include several kinds of insurance, contributions to retirement plans, partial payment of Social Security, and more. All these fringe benefits are specified at the time of employment. Tenured and tenure-track employees may be eligible for fringe benefits not offered to non-tenure-track employees.

In most instances both the institution and the employee make contributions to a retirement plan; to medical, dental, life, disability, and unemployment insurance; and to Social Security. Worker's compensation is another fringe benefit, the cost of which may be paid fully by the institution or shared by the institution and the employee. Further, many private institutions pay the college tuition of faculty members' children at either the home institution or selected other colleges and universities.

Other benefits, some of them *in kind* (other than money), are provided by some institutions, including moving expenses, housing, and expenses to professional meetings and conferences. Such benefits may not be offered to all employees. They may accrue only to sought-after faculty, to faculty in higher ranks, or to faculty who have negotiated such benefits.

Frequently there are choices among retirement plans. State college and university professors often are eligible for either a state retirement system or the Teachers Insurance and Annuity Association College Retirement Equities Fund (TIAA–CREF). Private college and university professors may have a choice between their institution's retirement plan or TIAA–CREF. When there is a choice, the alternatives should be examined carefully. One plan may vest sooner or provide better payoff than the other. *Vesting* means that both the employer's and the employee's contributions lock in after a specified number of years; the total contribution becomes the property of the professor, either at retirement or on transferring to another institution.

TIAA–CREF is transferable from one institution to another, provided that both institutions participate in it. More than 12,800 education and research institutions participated in TIAA–CREF in 2001. Whether transferability is important to a professor depends in part on whether he or she expects to move to another institution at some point during his or her career. New assistant professors beginning a career may not be able to predict such movement.

State-institution retirement plans cannot be transferred across state lines, but it often is possible to buy in to the system of a new state. Usually the number of years one can purchase is limited.

The contributions of employer and employee in a state or institutional retirement plan are invested by the managers of the plan. The participants in the plan have no options as to how or where the money is invested, except perhaps through a retirement board on which a few professors may serve. Subject to the policy of the employing institution, TIAA–CREF allows participants to allocate percentages of retirement funds among a variety of investment vehicles, such as money market funds, equity funds, bond funds, and real estate funds.

TWO-YEAR COLLEGES

Two-year institutions (community, technical, and junior colleges) are a giant operation, serving almost six million students. Less visible in American education than K–12 schools and four-year colleges and universities, they perform a multitude of functions not touched by either of those other types of institutions. The country's two-year colleges serve full- and part-time students in such areas as agriculture, architecture, business, communications, computer science, construction trades, engineering, health science, home economics, law, library science, precision production, protective services, and transportation, as well as arts and sciences. The two-year college offers vocational and preparatory programs. The latter are for study in the arts and sciences; students usually pursue them for transfer to four-year colleges or universities. Many students in two-year colleges attend only long enough to learn the skills necessary to qualify for a job. For others the two-year college is a second-chance institution, a place where they can try to qualify for admission to a four-year college or university after completing either one year of successful study or a two-year program. Many students at two-year colleges are older, and almost all are commuters; few two-year colleges have student housing.

Public two-year colleges have been among the fastest-growing institutions in American education. From 1972 to 1995, their number increased by more than 60 percent, and the number of associate degrees they conferred nearly doubled, from 292,000 to 536,000. In 1999 one-third of postsecondary institutions were public two-year colleges. These institutions employed almost one-third of the nation's higher education faculty and administration—and about two-fifths (44 percent) of all part-time faculty.

Two-year colleges are less likely than four-year colleges or universities to have administrative policies for evaluating the teaching of part-time faculty, and about one-fifth of them have made efforts to reduce their full-time faculty. Part-time faculty have far less access to retirement benefits than full-time faculty. They also are less likely to have union representation.

Two-year colleges are reviewed by regional accrediting agencies to ascertain general quality and by national specialty agencies in such fields as nursing, electronics, and engineering technology. Accreditation is one hallmark of quality that prospective faculty should check.

Anyone considering a career in two-year college teaching or administration should recognize the conflict that exists among two-year colleges about the purpose and the function of the institution. The differences were alluded to earlier. The main bone of contention is whether two-year colleges should favor the model of public schools or follow that of four-year colleges and universities regarding expectations for the academic preparation of staff, the role of faculty, tenure and rank, salary, and other matters. Obviously, the latter model has more status. Perhaps the public school model has more security and equality. Neither actually fits the two-year college, for it serves a diverse adult population and attends to a great variety of educational needs.

Teaching in Two-Year Colleges

The primary activity of two-year college faculty is teaching. Research and writing are not often expected. There is no pressure to "publish or perish."

The mode of operation is much like that of high schools. Evaluation of full-time faculty takes place during a two- or three-year probationary period, after which tenure is granted to those who have demonstrated adequacy. The procedures and the standards resemble those used in public schools. Some institutions have salary schedules that establish steps in each salary category, with the result that all full-time faculty with equal experience and comparable preparation earn the same salary. Categories are typically determined by levels of preparation, such as bachelor's degree, master's degree, master's degree plus thirty semester hours, and doctorate. Some two-year colleges have academic rank (that is, instructor, assistant professor, associate professor, and full professor); others do not. Two-year colleges draw faculty from a number of sources, but primarily from high schools and vocational-technical schools. Preparation for teaching in two-year colleges is not a set pattern of courses and degrees. Teachers of core subjects in the arts and sciences often come from high school teaching jobs. Their initial preparation has been for high school teaching. In many cases they have done graduate work in their major field. Other two-year college teachers come directly from university doctoral programs (with no preparation for teaching and no teaching experience), and their preparation has been more like that of the four-year college teacher.

Many of the occupational programs require teachers with craft, trade, and technical skills and experience. Such teachers often are drawn from the practitioners of the occupations they teach. Although the bachelor's degree is usually considered a minimum requirement and the master's degree often is necessary for regular or permanent employment, some vocational-technical staff do not have these academic credentials.

A few states have mandated minimum standards for preparation and licensure, insisting that all two-year college faculty, irrespective of teaching area, have an academic degree. Nonetheless, in those states a good number of vocational-technical people still teach with only their expertise as a credential.

Although two-year colleges are more like high schools than colleges in their criteria for faculty, their operational procedures, and their personnel practices, they are unique in the variety of adult students they serve and in institutional function. Two-year college teachers need more breadth in their subject field than high school teachers but not as much specialization as four-year college and university professors. Preparation in the art and science of teaching is highly desired and in some places required (which is not the case for four-year college and university teachers). Since 1950 a number of four-year colleges and universities have offered preparation programs for community and junior college teachers. Internships, not unlike student teaching, are required in some of them.

Administration in Two-Year Colleges

Administration in a two-year college is a cross between school and college administration. Because many two-year colleges have a number of the characteristics of the institutions above and below them in the education hierarchy, they inevitably reflect aspects of both types.

Two-year college administrators face more variety in the people and the circumstances they must deal with. The staff support that a two-year college administrator receives depends on the size and the budget of the college. Many community colleges operate with just a few administrators, whereas some of the larger institutions have an array of administrators similar to that in four-year colleges. The tasks to be accomplished are like those in any educational institution: hiring and maintaining a faculty, facilitating curriculum development and scheduling, overseeing building and equipment needs, supporting a guidance and counseling service, managing support staff, planning and monitoring a budget, maintaining a library or media center, operating a food service, and communicating with constituents, the community, and the press.

How all these jobs are executed by the top administrator and available staff differs from college to college. Usually there are departments and divisions, each headed by an administrator of some type.

Community, technical, and junior college administrators come largely from the public schools and two-year colleges. Many have been teachers in two-year colleges, and that is important because they understand the philosophy and the purpose of the two-year institution. Some have enrolled in graduate programs in two-year college leadership. Two-year college presidents, in particular, often are specifically prepared as administrators for two-year colleges. A number of major universities offer such programs, which culminate in a doctor's degree.

Career Patterns

Career patterns for people who stay in two-year colleges are much like those for high school personnel. For example, in institutions without academic rank, teachers secure tenure in the first few years on the basis of their effectiveness as teachers. Tenure does not depend on research and writing and does not require the doctorate.

The presence or the absence of academic rank in an institution is a factor that influences career pattern. Where there is academic rank, teachers go through evaluations for promotions in the way that four-year college teachers do, but with different criteria.

Whether or not they have academic rank, two-year colleges are apt to have a salary schedule, as public schools do, and to employ collective bargaining every few years to improve salary and working conditions.

The two-year college president serves at the pleasure of the board, usually on a contract but without tenure, much like a superintendent of schools. Two-year college presidents appear, however, to have longer terms than superintendents.

Finding Employment

The advice offered in Chapter 2 on finding employment as a teacher and in Chapter 3 on finding employment as an administrator applies to two-year-college job hunting. The best leads will be found in university placement offices. Positions also are advertised in journals and education newspapers.

Teachers, in particular, can inquire independently at college personnel offices and arrange to have their name placed on a list of people interested in employment. Some teachers begin as part-time instructors and are standing by when openings for full-time employment occur.

Two-year colleges have grown so much in the last twenty-five years that the demand for teachers has been constant. In fact, in the last decade, a number of candidates with earned doctorates who hoped to find positions at four-year colleges have taken jobs in two-year colleges, substantially increasing the percentage of teachers with doctorates on two-year college faculties.

Teachers and administrators in two-year colleges do not operate in a national market as senior college professors and administrators do. Hence the market for employment is more restricted to a state or a region.

Table 6.5 Average Salaries (in Dollars) of Two-Year College Professors on Nine-Month Contracts (in Dollars), by Control of Institution and Rank (Where Applicable), 2002

	Professor	Associate Professor	Assistant Professor	Instructor	Lecturer	No Rank
All institutions	60,803	47,967	42,667	35,421	41,687	39,685
Public	60,977	48,046	42,755	35,445	41,693	39,685
Private	52,678	46,662	42,228	34,948	38,938	NA

Source: From "Facts & Figures: Salaries of Professors," *Chronicle of Higher Education*, April 19, 2002, available at http://chronicle.com/chronicle/v48/4832guide.htm.

Salary and Fringe Benefits

Table 6.5 presents data on average salaries for two-year college faculty by control of institution and rank. Table 6.6 offers figures for selected administrative positions.

Fringe benefits in two-year colleges are like those in K–12 schools (see Chapter 2). The retirement system is a mix. Many colleges are part of state retirement systems. Others participate in TIAA–CREF, which, as noted earlier, is a portable pension system. It offers investment management, financial information and guidance, and a diverse selection of vehicles for building and receiving retirement income.

FIRSTHAND ACCOUNTS

Allen R. Warner is professor of curriculum and instruction at the University of Houston. He relates how he started his career.

> When I graduated from high school, I had neither the money nor the inclination to go to college. My parents had not even completed high school, so college seemed somewhat remote. My mother had dreamed of being an English teacher, but as the youngest of ten children in a northeast Indiana farm family, she fell victim to the conventional wisdom at the time that school was a waste for young girls. It was more important to find a nice young man and settle down, with both sets

Table 6.6 Median Salaries (in Dollars) of Selected Two-Year College
Administrators (in Dollars), 2002

Chief executive officer	122,000
Chief academic officer	88,294
Director, library services	55,370
Director, academic computing	59,451
Dean, arts and sciences	67,214
Dean, business	69,384
Dean, continuing education	70,371
Dean, education	71,282
Dean, engineering	66,648
Dean, fine arts	76,922
Dean, occupational or vocational education	68,857
Chief business officer	84,721
Chief financial officer	72,932
Chief personnel/human resources officer	65,468
Director, administrative computing	62,566
Chief development officer	63,900
Director, corporate and foundation relations	63,900
Chief public relations officer	55,438
Director, governmental relations	80,414
Director, community services	55,178
Chief student affairs officer	75,247
Chief admissions officer	58,072
Registrar	48,353
Director, food services	44,420
Director, student housing	38,040
Director, student activities	48,955
Director, student health services, nurse	48,673
Director, athletics	57,000

Source: Adapted from "Facts & Figures: Median Salaries of College Administrators
by Type of Institution, 2001–2002," *Chronicle of Higher Education*, April 12, 2002.

of parents setting the couple up with land, animals, a house, and a
barn. She was not allowed to go beyond the eighth grade. Instead of
accepting a rural existence, she took off for Chicago. Her unfulfilled
dream did tend to nag at me.

My high school graduation, though, occurred during the recession of 1961, and precious few jobs were available. The Army sounded like a reasonable idea (Vietnam being several years down the road), so I enlisted. In retrospect, that decision was one of my best. When my enlistment was complete, I took advantage of a state scholarship for veterans and the GI bill.

I began college as a twenty-one-year-old freshman business major, with an ambition to make as much money as possible. Within two years that ambition changed. Money, I realized, was not as important to me as making a contribution to society. I decided to teach, and I have never regretted the decision. More than thirty years later, I still love teaching.

I went on for a doctorate out of the same motivation to make a contribution. Although I thoroughly enjoyed teaching high school social studies, I realized that if I worked really hard, I might have a greater impact.

Since joining the University of Houston faculty, I have been blessed with opportunities both within the institution and at national and international levels.

For most of us who become professors—especially us former teachers who are used to having our time regulated by classroom bells—the hardest part is that we are, in the words of Jean-Paul Sartre, "condemned to freedom." We have to make many choices about how to use our time.

In general, professors are responsible for teaching, scholarship, and professional service. The balance among the three areas depends on the type of institution in which the professor is employed and his or her career stage. Professors normally spend six years on probation before being considered for tenure. The beginning rank for a "baby doc" is usually assistant professor, and often (but not always) promotion to associate professor and the granting of tenure are tied together. The ultimate is to be a tenured full professor.

Faculty in small, private institutions usually carry a heavier load of actual teaching than do their colleagues in larger research universities. Faculty in research universities, on the other hand, typically have to meet higher expectations in terms of published scholarship. Untenured faculty must spend more of their time establishing a scholarly record and demonstrating excellence in teaching. Senior, tenured faculty spend a proportionately greater amount of time providing service on university committees or providing leadership in professional organizations at the local, state, and national levels.

Even before being tenured, I was elected to the board of directors of the Association of Teacher Educators, a national professional group in which I had become involved as a graduate student. When I completed that term, I was asked to represent the association on the National Council for Accreditation of Teacher Education, the accrediting body in this country that is recognized by the U.S. Department of Education to provide national quality assurance for programs to prepare educators.

Both of these professional service roles proved to be exciting experiences as well as great personal honors. On the National Council for Accreditation of Teacher Education, I was part of decisions about whether teacher education institutions from across the country were worthy of the prestige that is accorded by national accreditation. In the field of education, state approval of teacher education programs is basic because each state issues its own licenses to practice in the teaching profession. National accreditation is voluntary (unless the state requires it), and it speaks highly of the institution that is willing to go above and beyond minimum state expectations in its teacher education programs.

Upsides and Downsides

A career in higher education, especially in preparing teachers and administrators, is a wonderful opportunity to have an impact on the future. If I send a new kindergarten teacher into the profession today, he or she will teach children who will live into the twenty-second century. That's impact!

Providing some measure of leadership in professional organizations at the national level is another form of impact. The Association of Teacher Educators began in 1920, and at this writing I have just completed a term as president of the association. Inheriting the legacy of others, and leaving a legacy of one's own, are special opportunities that few people have.

The major downside of a career as a professor is the prolonged apprenticeship that one must endure to be tenured in higher education. That six-year period can be full of angst and anxiety. Administration in higher education is professional service, and the mounds of memoranda I wrote over the years never have been solicited by a publisher. The journal articles, chapters, books, and papers I wrote and continue to write count far more as the coin of the realm in higher education.

Amy H. Shapiro is professor of philosophy at Alverno College in Milwaukee, Wisconsin, where she has been teaching since 1986. She describes what the work is like, what some of the upsides and downsides are, and what she would advise people seeking a position like hers.

My first experience teaching was at a small private school in a western suburb of Chicago. An introduction to moral philosophy gave me a glimpse of the extraordinary power of teaching. The course was for students in the health profession, most of whom were nurses. Moral philosophy came alive in the context of their everyday choices and responsibilities. Their wealth of experience and the profound issues they brought to questions of ethics created a dynamic that made every class session engaging and exciting for both the students and me. That dynamic also gave me a grasp of applied philosophy.

As a college professor, I never cease to be amazed at how ironic it is that the least of my professional time is spent teaching. Fortunately I work in a college that is truly devoted to teaching. As a result, I do not have the pressures to publish that many other faculty have. I am expected to play a significant role in curriculum design, in development of new faculty, and in ongoing dialogues with my colleagues about learning and assessment strategies; to sit on college committees; and to be actively involved in education-related issues in the community.

In a college where the focus is on the student, another important aspect of my job is involvement with student groups and concerns. In addition to my membership in my discipline division and department, I advise two student groups. I attempt to attend as many student programs or sports events as possible throughout the year, and

I sometimes am asked by student groups to participate in their programs. In a small college, faculty support of the extracurricular environment is extremely important. It helps maintain a sense of the value of student life apart from, though in support of, academics. It also allows students to be visible in roles other than those of just students in a classroom. This has probably taken on greater importance over the years because college students seem to have many more responsibilities outside of school than they used to and it is important to them for their families or significant others to meet their faculty and participate in college life.

In addition to the extracurricular dimensions of involvement in student life, my everyday tasks include such things as working with students in planning and applying to graduate schools, writing recommendations and evaluations (in addition to the countless amounts of feedback on papers and assignments), academic advising, and developing techniques for teaching students with learning disabilities.

Upsides and Downsides

In many ways the ups are the downs in teaching. I love the experience of watching my students learn and figuring out what will work best in the classroom. This can be enormously labor intensive, as it requires seeing each class as a new entity with new learning abilities and needs. And it requires configuring classroom processes to fit those abilities and needs. This calls for knowledge of educational processes above and beyond knowledge of the discipline, and it requires thinking about the multiple ways students might access disciplinary frameworks and conceptually grasp course concepts and texts.

Determining the best method of assessment and grading can be very trying and often very challenging. The excitement of creating a new assignment to meet the learning needs of students and to move them to a new level can be dashed to the ground on reading the first three papers. Alternatively, an assignment may be extremely useful with a few classes in a particular area and then suddenly flop. The flip side to this is to view a course as being only about the subject. The consequence is a kind of rote learning for students and locking most students out of an experience of epistemological insight with the exception of a few students. Classroom process and learning designs are powerfully challenging and demand that one reach beyond one's own discipline to think about how each student can gain an understanding and meet the outcomes of the course. When I am successful at accomplishing these goals, it is amazingly exciting and humbling at the same time.

Advice

Teaching has become a liberator for me. In the classroom I recognize a part of me that without teaching I don't seem to have access to. This part of me is boldly generous and abundantly open to ways of thinking and knowing. My love of teaching is based on the extraordinary student I become in the classroom. I think that good teachers have to be willing to be transformed, to be engaged with students on such a level that investment in their disciplines is relinquished to the possibility of seeing the discipline from countless possible points of view. But if one wants to be a teacher in higher education, then there are a number of expectations to set aside. Teaching, real devotion to teaching, is an ongoing and extremely intense process that demands a great deal of time, effort, and research. To be able to teach often requires that one put in one's dues and publish the requisite amount of articles and books before one can truly devote oneself to teaching. Alternatively, there are small private liberal arts schools and community colleges that view teaching as a valued and significant enterprise and therefore do not emphasize research over teaching as often as large universities do.

I cannot think of a life more rewarding than teaching at the college level. As I teach in an institution that is in an urban setting and is devoted to the education of women from the diverse communities in which it is situated, I find that I have been educated beyond what I had initially thought possible. I have been given the opportunity to imagine lives dramatically different from my own and to engage people I might otherwise never have met. Teaching and the learning that can happen in the classroom environment make possible the breakdown of barriers that often exist in other places of our lives. In the face of complex material and the need to develop intellectual abilities, learning becomes an incredible equalizer if the environment is created to view learning as an opportunity for all.

CHAPTER 7

ADULT AND CONTINUING EDUCATION

In its broadest conception, adult and continuing education (hereafter referred to simply as continuing education) encompasses any program of study offered to mature people who have completed their formal education and wish to pursue further learning. In this chapter, however, the definition is limited to work-related or leisure-oriented programs that are designed to benefit individual adults by promoting their career and profession or by enhancing their quality of life. It includes *inservice education*, a term commonly used in education to refer to individual professional development of K–12 and higher education personnel. Further, it covers professional development as a distinct category for people seeking further specialized training in law, the health professions, management, public administration, municipal and state government, and veterinary medicine. It also encompasses staff development for K–12 and higher education personnel because activities under this rubric, though designed to improve faculties and institutions, are client oriented, not profit oriented.

A broader definition of continuing education would include training that is intended exclusively or primarily to benefit an organization for its own sake or profit—for example, training that prepares an employee to perform his or her job more efficiently in order to increase the employer's profit margin, or training that teaches an employee new skills that he or she will apply in the workplace to improve service or productivity. That type of education is taken up in Chapter 8, under careers in business and industry.

Over the years, continuing education has had several labels, and new ones still are being created for it. This is understandable because the field is just emerging. A type of education that, according to Patricia Cross in *Adults as Learners*, "involves all kinds of people, learning all manner of subjects and skills, through all kinds of methods, from multiple providers" is bound to be in search of a name. Earlier in its history, it was called *nontraditional study* (which it was and is) and then *adult and continuing education* (which is more descriptive). Recently the terms *lifelong learning* and *lifelong education and learning* have been used.

With the successive name changes, the concept has grown. Initially the notion was to find ways of discovering what the adult learner wanted and then to provide it. As time passed and thoughtful people looked more closely at that concept, they realized that responding only to immediate needs was haphazard and fragmentary. Gradually a more holistic concept evolved. Now, among leaders in continuing education at least, the push is for a learning society in which men and women are the agents of their own education, in the context of a restructured traditional system and well-developed potential outside the existing system.

Continuing education encompasses a variety of activities. For example, some people seek basic literacy—the ability to read and write. School dropouts, realizing that a high school diploma is essential to securing a job, study to take the General Educational Development (GED) test. Immigrants from non-English-speaking countries study English as a second language. Secretaries learn word processing on a computer to gain a promotion. Thirty-five-year-olds who have not finished or even started college enroll in programs that grant credit for life and work experience, and advisers help them design individualized programs of study for a bachelor's degree. People who have helplessly witnessed a relative, friend, or stranger experience a heart attack take training in cardiopulmonary resuscitation (CPR).

Elderhostel programs for senior citizens also might be included. These programs, usually a week or two long and often held at a college or a university, are designed for learning of all types. Participants are typically in residence during the program in a continuing education center, at a conference center, or at some other site with appropriate accommodations. The purpose of the program is to provide stimulation, challenge, and enjoyment for people in the later years of life.

At the other end of the continuum, professionals find inservice education courses to update themselves on developments in their field. For example, a physician takes a short course to learn about new medications for hypertension; a dentist enrolls in a seminar on composite bonding (a process for joining a filling to a tooth); an assistant professor completes a workshop on inquiry-based teaching at her faculty center for teaching and learning; an interior designer participates in a weeklong institute on concepts in lighting; or a teacher attends a workshop on portfolio assessment.

Leisure-oriented continuing education features one-shot sessions and long-term programs on a multitude of subjects: omelet making, conversational Spanish, financial planning, computer programming, Chinese cooking, time management, parenting, picture framing, woodworking, and oil painting, to name just a few.

Somewhere between work- and leisure-related education are practical courses in coping with new tax laws, sessions on watching weight, classes in aerobics, training in new computer programs for personal accounting, and seminars on career planning.

Why is continuing education important and necessary? In a rapidly changing society, learning must be continuous. The education acquired in schools and colleges during childhood and youth will never again be adequate for a lifetime (if it ever was). In *Adults as Learners*, Patricia Ross observes, "Margaret Mead once remarked that the world in which we are born is not the world in which we will live, nor is that the world in which we will die." People constantly need to make useful additions to their knowledge, to renew or broaden their perspective, to revitalize their thinking. They need additional education to continue their personal growth and to keep abreast of new developments and discoveries.

Radical changes have occurred since World War II. Americans have learned to use and appreciate a variety of products and devices that they never had before, including frozen foods, television, jet airplanes, air conditioning, home computers, and DVD movies. Communication satellites, the Internet, robots, and E-mail have revolutionized industry, communications, and life in general. To accommodate and capitalize on these and other technological developments, people have had to acquire new knowledge, learn new skills, and adopt new attitudes. The impact of the changes has been seen in job losses, entirely new kinds of jobs and careers, changes in lifestyles, and moral and ethical conflicts. All these developments have ignited a rethinking of general education.

TRENDS IN PARTICIPATION

From 1991 to 1999, there was an overall increase in participation in continuing education. The increase was widespread, occurring among virtually every group of adults: all age groups except those thirty-five to forty-four years old, both women and men, all racial and ethnic groups, all education levels, all labor force groups, and all occupation groups except those in professional or managerial positions.

The increasing participation in adult education and the accommodations to change are far from complete. For example, many educators have not discovered how to work with the more mature learner. The modes of instructing children, youth, and young adults in schools and colleges are not as effective with their elders. How to alter teaching for mature people is only beginning to be explored in traditional education, and by just a few institutions. As well, there are troubling signs that some groups are being left behind, especially Hispanics, those with less education, those with lower-status jobs, and those who are employed part-time. Thus, although the increase in participation has been widespread, highly educated and high-status groups have been the most frequent beneficiaries of continuing education. Also, women are participating at a higher rate than men.

TYPES OF PROGRAMS

Continuing education takes place in all kinds of settings, with and through a variety of media. One prominent setting is the school or college campus, where continuing education is usually offered at hours when people who work have free time to attend—that is, evenings and weekends. It also is offered off campus, either with professors traveling to selected sites where instruction is given or with students studying independently at home. Community and junior colleges provide many continuing education courses and workshops. Community schools and individual school districts are another part of the continuing education enterprise.

Independent Learning

Independent-learning options for continuing education under school and college auspices appear to be increasing in importance and number. Correspondence courses, the open university, independent study, and distance learning are quite similar, yet different. A number of colleges, universities, and other education agencies offer some or all of these types of continuing education in almost any subject imaginable. Students may enroll for one course, or several courses over time, and then terminate their involvement; or they may enroll to earn a degree, which requires a planned program of courses. The possibilities in program type and content vary with the institution.

In correspondence courses the process takes place entirely by mail. Teachers and students never meet. Students receive materials, assignments, and requirements (which are typically standardized for all students taking the same offering) from an institution and work at their own pace. They periodically send in completed written work, which is critiqued and evaluated by staff at the institution. A final examination may be required.

Distance learning is much the same as independent study except that it is supported by the Internet. It is designed particularly for people in remote places and for those who must study at home. Study is guided and enhanced by print materials, teleconferencing transmissions, and Web-based content, which may take the form of lectures, demonstrations, dramas, photo essays, documentaries, case studies, panel discussions, and more. The institution sponsoring the distance learning provides and recommends materials for study and is responsible for evaluating student performance. Evaluation of work is by Web-based examination, written papers that are communicated electronically, and special projects.

Professional Development Programs

Local school districts are major sponsors of the development of their staff. Some of this kind of continuing education takes place on school time, with students being given a half or a full day off. In such sessions, staff are introduced to new curricula; oriented to new federal, state, and local policies affecting instruction; and familiarized with technological developments.

Intermediate and cooperative school districts also are providers of inservice and continuing education for school personnel and sometimes for parents and other citizens. These organizations are groups of public school districts banded together to provide services that single districts cannot afford.

Teacher centers and professional development centers, most commonly operating under school district auspices, are fairly recent innovations in this country (imported from England) for the continuing education of teachers and other professional school personnel. A hallmark of teacher centers is that they respond to the needs and the requests of teachers. They serve teachers with quick help in one-shot sessions, but they also provide workshops and other activities that involve long-term, in-depth study. The site of activity is usually the teacher center, which keeps its doors open late afternoons, evenings, and Saturdays. Teacher centers in many places have enlarged their role. They have become professional development centers, the name change signaling accommodation of a broader school audience. Recently, professional development center staff have begun working onsite at the building level to facilitate school improvement.

Regional educational laboratories are another provider of continuing education, largely for elementary and secondary school teachers. Created and funded by the federal government and spread across the country, they are charged with improving education through special projects that articulate research findings addressing perennial and current problems in education. Typically, laboratory personnel develop materials, models, protocols, and methods that provide strategies and content to remedy a particular problem.

Professional associations and societies, including teacher unions, conduct three basic types of continuing education:

1. Programs that provide instruction to further the organizational commitment of the group
2. Programs designed for the professional development of individuals belonging to the group
3. Pilot projects with schools and colleges preparing education personnel, to promote innovation in practice

In the first category, there is direct or indirect orientation, indoctrination, and sometimes training. For example, a union may provide programs on collective bargaining and political action; a science teachers association may hold workshops on promoting the importance of science in school programs; and a language teachers association may conduct seminars on advancing the cause of educating Americans in a second language. In the second category, associations and societies conduct conferences, workshops, and other inservice education programs to acquaint teachers and administrators with new content and procedures in their respective fields. In the third category, selected schools or colleges (or both) engage in grassroots reform and experimentation, identifying problems and experimenting with possible solutions.

Proprietary schools usually focus on business, accounting, and secretarial training. Although most of them are postsecondary institutions, they are open to people of any age who seek new skills and knowledge in business, banking, and office procedures.

DANTES

The U.S. Department of Defense sponsors the Defense Activity for Non-Traditional Education Support (DANTES), a voluntary education program for active-duty military and reserve personnel. Through contracts and agreements with a variety of institutions and agencies, DANTES offers diverse programs of adult education and distance education. The military services provide tuition assistance to pay a percentage of the charges of an educational institution for the member to enroll in courses of study during off-duty time. The amount of money for support is uniform across the military services. Members of any branch of the armed forces are eligible.

The programs are comparable to those available to citizens outside the military and are available regardless of the service person's duty location. They are provided by accredited postsecondary vocational and technical schools, colleges, and universities.

Participating service members receive guidance and counseling services from qualified personnel so that they can make the most efficient use of government resources and the most effective use of their own time, money, and effort. About 300,000 DANTES–sponsored examinations are administered each year to military personnel.

Participants have opportunities to acquire basic educational and academic skills that are essential to successful job performance and new learning. Outside the United States, adult education programs are available to both service members and their adult family members. Among the services and programs are the following:

1. Examinations
2. Distance learning
3. Military evaluations
4. Service Members Opportunity Colleges

All take place outside the formal classroom.

The *examinations* program enables service personnel, no matter where they are located—aboard a ship, at remote stations, or stateside—to test for a high school equivalency (GED) credential or for credit that can apply toward a college degree. Further, through agreements with about thirty-two professional groups, such as the American Medical Technologists, the American Nurses Association, the American Speech-Language-Hearing Association, the Institute for the Certification of Engineering Technicians, and the National Association of Social Workers, service people can take professional certification examinations to demonstrate skills learned in the military.

Through *distance learning*, 6,000-plus high school, undergraduate, and graduate correspondence courses are available from forty-five regionally accredited colleges and universities.

The *military evaluations* program is conducted in cooperation with the American Council on Education, which arranges for evaluations of military courses and experiences and makes recommendations regarding the acceptance of them for credit.

More than 1,200 colleges and universities (a threefold increase since 1995) now constitute the network known as *Service Members Opportunity Colleges (SOC)*. These institutions have formulated policies and implemented programs to make higher education more accessible to military personnel. Hundreds of thousands of service members and their family members enroll annually in programs offered by SOC member universities, colleges, community colleges, and technical institutes.

Graduate School, USDA

The Graduate School of the U.S. Department of Agriculture (USDA) is a continuing education school offering career-related courses to all adults, regardless of education or place of employment. Annually the Graduate School provides more than 2,500 courses for career development and personal enrichment in upwards of 100 cities. Classes are designed to help people realize their career potential, improve their job performance, and enrich their lives. More than 350 employees and 1,200 instructors are drawn from government, business, and academe. As experts in their field, Graduate School instructors bring a practical focus to the classroom. In 2001, more than 180,000 persons received training.

The school was created in 1921 by Secretary of Agriculture Henry C. Wallace to provide continuing education for young research scientists of the USDA. Wallace believed that a graduate school would help attract and retain qualified personnel at a time (shortly after World War I) when the demand for them was acute. The school soon expanded to serve other government personnel. Today the name Graduate School reflects whom the school serves rather than what it does. It continues to serve adults—both government employees and the general public—who have graduated from full-time schooling.

Although it is affiliated with the USDA, the Graduate School is completely self-supporting, receiving no funding from the government. Its present mission is to increase the efficiency, the effectiveness, and the productivity of government organizations through training and related services and to assist individuals in improving their job performance and pursuing lifelong learning.

CONTINUING EDUCATION STAFF

Three categories of staff are the most prominent in continuing education: teachers, administrators, and counselors. The configuration of faculty in continuing education varies greatly with the type and the structure of the institution or the agency. In the college or university, regular tenured faculty teach courses in continuing education as part of their normal load, or as an overload for extra pay. Also, *adjunct professors*—that is, people who serve part-time while holding full-time jobs elsewhere—teach courses in their areas of expertise and experience. Thousands of faculty function in one or the other of these teaching categories. They serve as advisers to degree candidates and special students. The effort is to help people who work full-time to upgrade their skills and knowledge or earn an academic credential. Frequently an institution of higher education has a specific college or office of continuing education.

Often the full-time staff in continuing education at colleges and universities are the administrators or the coordinators of the program. (The exception is community and junior colleges, where many full-time faculty may devote all of their time to continuing education and where special counselors may assess interest, ability, and aptitude to advise students in educational and career planning.) The job of administrative staff is to ascertain the training needed by particular populations, create courses, hire instructors, handle logistics (place, day, and time of the courses), provide assistance in teaching methodology (for outside experts who teach infrequently or have never taught), market courses, pilot-test new courses, and evaluate the effectiveness of courses offered.

Counselors are important staff members, especially to adults returning to college after an extended time away. Senior colleges and universities are less apt to designate counselors to advise mature adults in educational and career planning. The counselor plays an important role in guidance, admission, retention, evaluation, and other functions that facilitate the student's understanding of his or her potential and the offerings that can contribute to achieving that potential.

In professional associations and societies, the staff of the organization often serve in the capacity of teacher or manager (or both) of continuing education programs, usually for part of their workload. Many have been teachers or professors in prior positions. Some of the most skilled planners of continuing education are organization staff. They plan and conduct innumerable workshops. The conferences they design and carry out are, in most instances, continuing education. Being privy to the thinking and the planning that organization staff give to every detail of a workshop or a conference—purposes, content, participants, speakers, logistics, materials, marketing, and evaluation—is a lesson in highly sophisticated continuing education.

Teachers' Duties

Two-thirds to three-quarters of the 500,000-plus teachers in continuing education work part-time. Many hold another teaching or administrative job full-time or part-time, or they are homemakers, craftspeople, artists, or participants in other walks of life who can contribute resources, knowledge, and skills to adult learning.

Teaching at any level includes planning curriculum, assembling and preparing materials and techniques, instructing, demonstrating techniques, reading student assignments, preparing and giving examinations, attending to such clerical details as reporting grades, and participating in faculty meetings (see the discussion of teaching in Chapter 2). However, continuing education is different from other postsecondary teaching in some significant ways. Because participation is voluntary, continuing education is more concerned with the learner, with fashioning content and methods to fit the individual; thus it functions at the cutting edge of education. Among the goals of continuing education are to make learning more self-directed, to build attitudes and skills that make learning lifelong, and to use diverse providers—that is, any person, institution, or organization that can contribute to learning.

In the best circumstances, continuing education employs more and better techniques of teaching. There is lecturing, but teachers strive to facilitate learning rather than direct it; to engage students in problem solving, practical applications, demonstrations, discussion, and independent learning; and to give attention to the motivations and the learning styles of adults. There is more conferring with students and more time spent discovering a student's level of achievement, capability, study habits, and command of basic skills. Also, teachers refer students to counselors more often for assessment of abilities, capacities, and aptitudes and for educational and career planning.

Working Conditions

Teachers in correctional, literacy, and community-based continuing education programs spend three to thirty hours a week in classes, and they carry heavy teaching loads—as high as six to nine hours per day, several days per week. That situation is not true of four-year college and university professors involved in continuing education, however. They carry the traditional teaching load in higher education, generally twelve to fifteen semester hours in colleges, six to twelve semester hours in universities, with only part of it in continuing education.

In most situations, teaching takes place in the late afternoon, in the evening, or on the weekend, and it ranges from one-shot sessions of two to three hours to courses that run the full semester, meeting one to three times a week.

Preparation

When continuing education "[involves] learning on the part of people of all ages and from all walks of life using the multiple learning resources of society to learn whatever they want or need to know" (as phrased in *Adults as Learners*), specifying how teachers should be prepared is difficult. Certainly they will not all have qualifications similar to those for teaching in traditional schools and colleges. Many continuing education teachers are selected for their special expertise and experience in a subject, trade, art, craft, or profession that they practice or teach in a full-time job. As a consequence, faculty in continuing education are a diverse group.

Most teachers have skills and knowledge developed through experience or formal education, frequently both. The bachelor's degree is usually a minimum requirement, except with artisans whose experience has made them experts. Many continuing education teachers have a master's degree or a doctorate. Some states require a credential, a license, or a certificate from the appropriate professional group; other states require licensure as a teacher. Criteria often are flexible, particularly in areas not commonly taught in academe.

Career Patterns

The path of advancement in continuing education is probably only from teaching to administration, if that indeed is advancement. Of course, programs come in many sizes, and one form of advancement is progression to more responsible, more challenging jobs. Larger programs in wealthier schools, colleges, universities, and associations have more prestige and pay better than those in smaller, less affluent organizations. That route is more open to administrators and coordinators than to teachers and counselors, although becoming a professor of continuing education at a large, prestigious university represents advancement, particularly if the person started out in a school district's evening studies program. Moving into university-level theoretical work or research in continuing education also may be an advancement. The hierarchy for advancement aside from these steps is limited (except for those who shift into or shuttle in and out of assignments in business and industry, as described in Chapter 8), partly because continuing education is less formalized than most other kinds of education and partly because it often is an adjunct operation.

Finding Employment

Because of the nature of teaching in continuing education, people often slip into it rather than prepare for it. Some teachers are sought by administrators of continuing education because their reputation has spread or their specialty is needed. In other instances, people themselves seek out opportunities, from interest in lifelong learning or from a desire to help people who need a second chance.

For teachers wanting employment in continuing education in two-year colleges, using the placement office of the college or university from which they graduated is an effective avenue. Personnel in most state departments of education are knowledgeable about sources of inservice employment. The most obvious approach is to make direct contact with the institutions in which one hopes to work. Some directors also are open to suggestions for new courses meeting the needs of the community and will consider proposals from experienced teachers or professionals proficient in their field.

An understanding of the purposes and the philosophy of continuing education is essential for a person seeking employment in the field. That understanding must be deeper and more comprehensive than can be conveyed in a chapter such as this. Courses and programs on continuing education and adult learning are offered in many universities, and the literature in the area is rich. Selected books are included in the Bibliography. The American Association for Adult and Continuing Education and the National University Continuing Education Association are other sources of information.

Salary and Fringe Benefits

Salary and fringe benefits in continuing education depend on whether the teacher, the counselor, or the administrator is part-time or full-time. The issue is more relevant for teachers because counselors and administrators are usually full-time, if not in continuing education, then at least in another position at the institution offering the continuing education.

Because many continuing educators also are teachers, counselors, or administrators in more formal educational contexts who have part-time responsibilities in continuing education, salaries and fringe benefits for them closely resemble those described in Chapters 2, 3, 5, and 6. The salaries and fringe benefits of artisans, craftspeople, tradespeople, and other adjunct and part-time personnel who are sought out for their special expertise are so diverse as to defy description. Experience and formal education, of course, are factors in salary determinations. But so is the sponsor of a particular program. For example, a community-based continuing education program for refugees, run by a volunteer group, may pay very meager salaries because it has very few funds and because teachers feel their work is a contribution to a cause.

Adjunct personnel are rather poorly rewarded in general, and they do not qualify for fringe benefits. That condition exists because institutional policy usually does not provide such benefits for anyone who is not a full-time employee. Few continuing education teachers complain, because they are covered for insurance and retirement benefits in full-time jobs. They can afford to teach for a salary without fringe benefits. For some the motivation is extra money; for others, teaching a course is a diversion from regular responsibilities, a chance to share ideas with people, or just fun. Salaries for adult and continuing education teachers working part-time (teaching one course) run from almost nothing to $6,000. In full-time employment, the range is $35,000 to $60,000. Information about salaries and fringe benefits for full-time college or university employment in continuing education is contained in Chapter 6.

FIRSTHAND ACCOUNT

Jean Fleming is a member of the graduate education program at College of the Southwest in Hobbs, New Mexico. A practicing educator since 1975, she holds a doctorate in educational leadership and policy studies from the University of Northern Colorado and a master's degree in adult education from Colorado State University. She discusses how she entered the field and offers advice to those interested in it.

Two years after graduating with my bachelor's degree in anthropology, I began volunteering as a tutor in citizenship, English as a second language, and reading at the Volunteers ClearingHouse in Fort Collins, Colorado. This community agency worked cooperatively with the local school district to serve educationally and economically at-risk adults, many of whom had come to the United States from Mexico. Over the next five years, I held a variety of positions with the clearinghouse and the school district, including ESL instructor, citizenship program coordinator, volunteer tutor coordinator of the local Right to Read program, and eventually coordinator of the jointly sponsored Adult Basic Education program.

Like many adult educators, I have spent my career in myriad positions. After fifteen years of experience, I decided to study for my doctorate. I graduated with an Ed.D. in educational leadership and policy studies, with an emphasis in adult education, from the University of Northern Colorado. After this, I embarked on a search for a tenure-track position in adult education. Within a year I joined the faculty of the Adult and Community Education graduate program at Ball State University in Indiana. Later I served as a visiting professor for a semester at the University of Tennessee.

After a three-year distance relationship with my husband, I made a career decision based on personal reasons. We moved to Hobbs, a small town in New Mexico, to support my husband's career, and I obtained a position as an assistant professor of graduate education at College of the Southwest.

Advice

A career in adult education, be it continuing education, community education, higher education, popular education, or any number of variations on the theme, is most frequently marked by both variety and commitment—a variety of work in a variety of places, all of it characterized and somehow unified by a foundational commitment to adult learners and adult learning.

The field at times is maddening and is itself perhaps only a state of mind: we struggle with issues of identity, and if you need a career that is clearly defined and delimited, adult education is not the career for you. Adult educators are never really sure of their jobs: we may be the first ones let go from our positions, our programs may be cut more readily than others, and funding for our jobs may come to an end depending on current governmental priorities. If a lucrative, steady paycheck for life is your goal, then adult education may not be a viable choice.

But if you love knowing you can have virtually unlimited opportunities to make a difference in the lives of harried, challenging, fascinating adults of any age, then the life of an adult educator can look pretty good. If you love being defined by your beliefs and not by your job responsibilities, adult education may intrigue you. If you believe that working with children, although vitally important, is not the only contribution an educator can or should make, then investigating adult education might prove worthwhile.

CHAPTER 8

EDUCATION IN BUSINESS AND INDUSTRY

In retail businesses, factories, and offices such as IBM, Safeway, General Electric, and Daimler Chrysler, education—or *training and development*, as it is called in the private sector—is a staple activity. The pace of innovation and adaptation in technical, manufacturing, and service organizations has been phenomenal. Robots, computers, lasers, and other developments in technology, including *E-learning* (learning via the Internet and other electronic means), have brought about a critical need to retrain technical employees. Constantly changing, more sophisticated approaches to marketing have necessitated the upgrading of personnel. Experimentation and findings in personnel management, training, and ways to promote employee growth have created a wholly new field: human resource development.

Other events that have given impetus to education in the private sector are foreign competition and the emergence of the employee as a company partner. The rising industrial prowess of foreign countries, many with much cheaper labor costs, has devastated or emasculated some basic industries in the United States, brought about the firing of many in the workforce, and created the need to retrain thousands of employees for new jobs. The realization that employees need cultivation, involvement, nurturing, and support to function well and productively has redirected the focus of the business and industrial training effort from a concentration on skills alone to a broad concern with employee development.

Training new employees, upgrading veteran workers, and introducing new techniques, technologies, and tactics—all that amounts to big business. The introduction of computers alone has created myriad changes. For example, in engineering, innumerable mechanical engineers have had to be reoriented to electrical engineering. Retraining that is less sophisticated but encompasses many more people has taken place with clerical and accounting employees. In a brief period, the computer has transformed offices, not only by replacing the typewriter but also by radically changing how data are aggregated, stored, duplicated, and presented.

The existence of private-sector careers in training and development is one of the best-kept secrets in American society. That is difficult to understand, given that thousands of people are teaching in the private sector and huge sums of money are being spent in the effort. It is predicted that three-fourths of all currently employed workers will need retraining throughout the twenty-first century. During this century, millions of manufacturing jobs will be restructured.

The American Society for Training and Development (ASTD) is one of the best sources of information on employer-provided workplace learning and the educators who train employees. It annually surveys trends in workplace learning and performance. The 2002 report *State of the Industry* says that private-sector employers spent $54.2 billion on formal training. The highest expenditures were in finance, insurance, and real estate; transportation and public utilities; and technology. On the basis of spending per eligible employee, nondurable manufacturing spent the most.

In 2000, in the 367 organizations (out of 1,000) that responded to ASTD's survey, about 87 percent of eligible employees in the civilian workforce received formal employer-provided training. Among eligible employees the greatest needs for training were information technology skills, managerial/supervisory skills, technical processes and procedures, occupational safety, and product knowledge.

Training in business and industry is conducted almost entirely for the benefit of the organization—that is, for what it will do to improve employee performance, productivity, service, and profit. Training runs the gamut from upgrading the skills and work style of technicians and blue-collar workers to training supervisors and executives in better, more efficient, more effective methods of management.

Leaders in business and industry also recognize the need to restore pride in work and product. That goal becomes even more important when team building—that is, learning to work cooperatively with other people—proves to be an important factor in the quality of production or service.

Education offered in the private sector is different from that offered in formal and more traditional institutions of education. It has not been formalized in content or ritual. It taps many disciplines and responds continuously to changing demands and new developments. It may be for orientation, safety and health, basic skills, workplace-related matters, job skills, or apprenticeship. The delivery system is shifting, but not as rapidly as anticipated. From 1994 to 1995, classroom- and lecture-based delivery declined from 78 to 69 percent. In 1998, organizations projected that by 2000, more than 20 percent of training would be delivered by technology or E-learning. However, the average amount of E-learning reached only 8.8 percent in 2000. Meanwhile, instructor-led training in the classroom increased from 77.6 percent in 1997 to 79.4 percent in 2000. Predictions for greater use of technology, particularly E-learning, still are high. However, materials and approaches, the needed know-how to produce programs, and the skills in using technology have not developed rapidly. As a consequence, the projection of more than 20 percent may not be realized soon.

The context of education in business and industry also makes it different from education in traditional institutions. The product or the service has been identified. The motive is profit. The purpose is clear, although ever changing. But a growing phenomenon is executives' and managers' awareness that their employees are people, not robots. This emerging recognition is not rooted in idealism; it is primarily practical. Employers and administrators are learning fast that employees are a resource, if motivated properly, involved adequately, and rewarded appropriately. They are central to the quality and the quantity of an organization's product or service. Life on the job is more pleasant for employees who feel a part of the larger enterprise. When they are involved in planning, they begin to care more about their accomplishments. Workers who interact harmoniously with peers come to like their work, are less fearful of change, and cooperate more effectively. Proponents of this philosophy, such as Thomas J. Peters and Robert H. Waterman, Jr. (authors of *In Search of Excellence* and other books on the subject), have made a reputation (and a fortune) researching and disseminating it.

The context is different, too, in areas influenced by technological development. Almost every year, jobs can call for different knowledge and skill. Innovation may require accommodation and new skills. Sometimes, complete retraining is necessary because an existing process or technology has become obsolete, irrelevant, or less competitive. An example is the advent of microcomputers, software for electronic typesetting, and laser printers, which together have made desktop publishing possible and thus have challenged conventional typesetting. The skills and the knowledge needed to operate new technologies often are completely different from those required to run former systems, even though the product may be much the same.

The goal of the trainer of technical and service employees is to develop new skills and competencies, build attitudes of interest and acceptance, ensure healthy relationships, and promote improved procedures. The more progressive companies also have trainers who counsel individual employees on managing change, on future job opportunities, and (sometimes) on personal problem solving. Training for supervisors and managers includes some of these topics, but it more often is focused on tasks and authority, strategies and philosophy, management and supervision, and organization and assignment of responsibilities across an enterprise.

WHAT BEING A TRAINER IS LIKE

ASTD has described fifteen functions that trainers perform:

1. Evaluating
2. Facilitating groups
3. Counseling individuals
4. Preparing written learning and instructional materials
5. Instructing
6. Managing training and development
7. Marketing
8. Producing media
9. Analyzing needs
10. Administering
11. Designing programs
12. Strategizing (developing long-range plans for the training and development organization)
13. Analyzing tasks
14. Theorizing (developing and testing theories of learning, training, and development)
15. Coaching application (helping individuals apply their learning)

Trainers usually have a repertoire of skills and abilities, among them several of the fifteen functions just identified. They modify and apply technologies and approaches to satisfy the purposes of a particular training session.

Several of the fifteen functions reveal a philosophy of training. The contrast with the philosophy of adult and continuing education described in Chapter 7 is striking. Philosophies are never pure, however, nor are they consistent in each camp.

There is more than a bit of glitz in this field, and it can become heady stuff for the most successful. That the trainer is flown to a session in the corporate jet and is paid $1,800 per day leaves the educators described in other chapters envious or resentful, if not suspicious. They look askance at the gimmicks, the profit motive, and the sometimes rah-rah approach of training and development. However, they rarely take a hard look, and they seldom recognize that this kind of education is part of free enterprise. Facilitating team building, helping managers analyze and solve performance issues, or transforming order takers into problem solvers translates into greater profits. The results make a difference in production and service costs, employee efficiency and morale, and the quality of products or services.

One trainer confides, "School and college teachers just don't realize how much we pack into sessions. This is really a very tightly organized kind of training. And it's much more bottom-line oriented than schools. If the corporate people don't see us making a difference, we've had it."

According to *Careers in Training and Development*, trends in training and development that will probably gain momentum in the next decade are as follows:

1. Development of human capital is becoming a goal of more organizations in response to the global threat of competition.

2. Education in organizations is being driven by needs—strategic goals and internal organizational issues—and is developing different thinking styles for improving and managing performance.

3. Corporations are becoming training institutions, and job-related learning is becoming more important than formal education in determining what a person does.

4. Organizations are developing new cultures for managing the performance of individuals and teams.

5. Training is a growth industry, and the key influences contributing to this growth are changing technologies and human assets being recognized for productive growth.

PREPARATION FOR BECOMING A TRAINER

There is no pat answer to the question of preparation for this career, and no one route to follow. A number of people in training and development have credentials and experience in the field of organizational development, and formal education in organizational development is available. However, there is more to training and development than just organizational development. Further, success may depend on whether a person seeks a job inside a company or hopes to operate as a freelancer.

People who find employment in training and development inside an organization often begin in another capacity with the company and move quite naturally into a training role. They may teach others about a job they have done or are doing, or they may informally help others learn. In this vein, experienced computer programmers induct new programmers, top salespeople share techniques and methods with other sales representatives, and veteran stockbrokers break in new members of the firm. A fairly common practice these days, when the trainer is an employee, is to assume the role of trainer for a specified period and then rotate back into other corporate, service, or manufacturing duties. Once in the role, trainers often seek outside instruction for themselves or attend conferences and workshops to gain additional skills. Learning new knowledge or skills on the job, planning and conducting training sessions, and getting feedback from participants (and management) provide chances to refine competence further.

Becoming a freelance trainer—that is, one who works on contract with businesses and industries—happens in a number of ways. Many freelance trainers start as teachers in schools or colleges, often earning a graduate degree in those roles. They also may participate in several special training sessions themselves with groups that specialize in training and development or organizational development, such as ASTD and the National Training Laboratories. Once they become employees of a school system or an institution of higher education, they find opportunities for outside work as trainers, or they become consultants to university departments of industrial management, business administration, and community planning. Both avenues lead to other assignments. Reputations spread quickly and easily for quality trainers. The bottom line is results. Achieving them builds trust, which easily grows into contract renewals for the same or other types of training. Whether participants are workers or managers, when a trainer makes a difference, everyone knows it.

One critical recognition in training adults is that employees are mature people. They cannot be treated otherwise. Trainers who have come out of teaching in schools and colleges must be aware that adult learning has its peculiarities, its uniqueness.

Trainers also must have an awareness of the business and industrial world and be conversant with its problems and issues. For educators shifting from academe, that means becoming current with business literature and news by reading such publications as the *Wall Street Journal*, *Business Week*, and *Fortune*.

Like most professionals, trainers have networks. They know many of their counterparts inside and outside organizations. Establishing and maintaining a network is essential not only for the freelance trainer but also for the insider, because more than employment prospects flow through a network. Networks channel ideas, information, and access to resources.

If a person has something to offer, becoming part of a network of trainers is easy. To remain in it, though, one must be able to interact creatively with other trainers. Networks are invisible webs connecting people who know and trust one another and among whom continuous give-and-take occurs. In the give-and-take, there is a tender balance. A person dares not give overzealously or take too much. Among trainers particularly, reciprocity is essential. Networking may be one of the most important kinds of involvement a trainer can have.

FINDING EMPLOYMENT AS A TRAINER

Some people are more comfortable in a salaried position than in a freelance operation. Such jobs are usually full-time within an organizational setting. Other people are happier with the independence (and risk) of freelancing. Whichever type one chooses, having a career means finding work and keeping it. In training and development, the route to employment is as nebulous as a prescription for preparation is. As already indicated, most trainers have a college education but not necessarily as educators or trainers. Their interest in training and development may occur well after college. Charting the way is very much an individual matter. It means making a careful assessment of talents, abilities, and needed skills and competencies. It means finding ways to hone existing assets and acquire new ones. Exploring course work and other kinds of preparation available through colleges and universities, interviewing professionals in training and development, and becoming informed about other agencies and institutions that specialize in this area are good first steps. The labels to look for are *human development*, *human resource development*, *career development*, *organizational development*, and *corporate development*. The word *training* may appear in any of them. ASTD gives the following advice to people planning a career in training and development:

1. Establish goals and keep them flexible.
2. Anticipate several careers during a lifetime.
3. Make life planning a part of career planning.
4. Write down your personal and professional values and philosophy.
5. Create an image of your desired future—look ahead three to five years.
6. Assess your present career situation and look at your preferred future.
7. Elicit feedback from your colleagues to critique, update, and revise your plan.
8. Decide in advance that you will manage your own training and development.

SALARY AND FRINGE BENEFITS

The payoffs for trainers in business and industry are many. The satisfaction and the excitement of seeing people and situations change (provided that the effort goes well) may be the two most prominent benefits. Participation in an emerging field and high visibility are others.

Salaries and fees vary considerably. Top trainers, be they employees or freelancers, have incomes in the category of company executives. Internal generalists and specialists in design and development receive salaries of $200 to $350 per day. A considerably wider range is paid to freelancers: $500 to $3,000 per day.

As for fringe benefits, trainers employed full-time by an organization have the same fringe benefits as other employees. Freelancers must provide their own health insurance, retirement equity, and leave.

Employment as a trainer is high-risk work from the standpoint of job security. When corporate budgets are cut, training often is one of the first areas to see reductions. On the other hand, freelance consultants may benefit at such times because organizations can use them without the expense of benefits and without the obligation of long-term employment.

FIRSTHAND ACCOUNT

Ron Gager is a management consultant working out of Boulder, Colorado. He graduated from Central Michigan University in Mount Pleasant, Michigan, with a degree to teach biology and chemistry. Later he earned a Master of Education degree at the University of Colorado at Boulder. He was a classroom teacher for eight years. He relates how he got started in training and development, describes some of the upsides of the work, and offers advice.

My journey from the high school classroom to the corporate boardroom was never planned, or even part of an educated hunch that teaching biology was going to be in any way linked to the work I now do in the corporate arena. In fact, teaching human anatomy and physiology to bright, eager eleventh and twelfth graders was all I really wanted to do after college. I might still be doing that if it wasn't for a chance dealt to me in the early 1970s to become a certified Outward Bound instructor within my school district's newly formed adaptation of the Outward Bound principles to the classroom and beyond.

That experience, which included helping develop the district's first Senior Seminar (a semester-long experiential learning alternative for seniors) and spending many summers instructing and directing courses for the Colorado Outward Bound School, set the stage for my adventures as an educator and as a consultant. Along the way I was fortunate to be linked with Eliot Wiggington of Foxfire fame in an effort to help teachers across the nation adapt the experiential concepts of both Foxfire and Outward Bound through hands-on teacher training workshops. This first taste of consulting whetted my appetite for working with adults and eventually led me into the teacher center movement, first as the director of the Learning Exchange in Kansas City, Missouri, and later as a consultant to the National Education Association's national teacher center initiative.

Although I initially missed the excitement of seeing high schoolers discover the magic in scientific inquiry, I reveled in helping adults make similar discoveries about teaching and learning. A highlight of those years was a presentation I made on experiential learning to Ph.D.s at the Educational Testing Service in Princeton, New Jersey. I began by having them all tape their thumbs across their palms and then try to complete a dozen "great thumbless survival tests," like opening a can of soup with a typical opener. What a thrill to see these very capable academics wrestle first with a can opener and a can and later with the challenge of articulating the learning process that formed the basis for the activity (which taught key concepts about the evolution of the opposable thumb in primates).

I found my way from the world of teacher education to corporate training and development via my role as director of Colorado Outward Bound's leadership development program for corporate teams. One corporate client, Xerox, offered me the chance to become part of their internal cadre of management trainers, and I began a career as a corporate training manager in the early 1980s. After a range of positions at Xerox, I joined a newly acquired Division of Air Products and Chemicals as its director of training and organizational development and gained additional skills in the training and organizational effectiveness fields. Three years later I started my own management consulting practice and now am in my sixteenth year as a consultant to corporations and their leaders and teams.

Upsides

Highlights of my practice include being part of the consulting team that helped Jack Welch at General Electric create a culture based on "speed, simplicity, and self-confidence" and participating in similar efforts at J.P. Morgan, Sears, Disney, and General Motors. I had the good fortune to work with consultants and academics who were "writing the book" on organizational improvement. Today my work is centered on a Six Sigma (statistical quality improvement) effort at Telstra, the Australian telephone company, and on helping a large engineering services firm in the States figure out how to grow profitably in an ever-changing, highly competitive marketplace.

Advice

If you are interested in consulting in the private sector, first get some good experience and training in education, and then make the transition to working with adults. Be willing to change your orientation to the interests of the for-profit world by becoming familiar with periodicals and newspapers on business and organizations. Be interested in people and organizations, have a sense of humor, and be able to deal with ambiguity and change. Finally, remember that learners come in all shapes and sizes and that even corporate CEOs of great renown started out life as eager kindergartners trying to write their name in finger paints.

CHAPTER

9

CAREERS IN GOVERNANCE AND CONTROL OF EDUCATION

At the top of the education pyramid, at the state and national levels, are careers in governance and control of education—in state boards and departments of education, federal education agencies, professional councils and associations, membership groups, and other agencies listed in the Appendix. Most of the people in these units have come up through the ranks. They are drawn from the various institutions described in Chapters 2 through 7. Most are appointed; some are elected. These positions are included as careers because that is what most of them have become. In only a few positions are the holders expected to rotate in and out on a three-, four-, or five-year schedule.

Perhaps the best way to suggest what careers in the top professional and government bureaucracies are like is to describe the roles of these agencies and associations and some of the duties of the professionals who staff them.

STATE BOARDS AND STATE DEPARTMENTS OF EDUCATION

The control of public education rests with the states. Thus there are fifty separate systems of education. Almost every state has a state board of education that has authority to establish policies, rules, and regulations for carrying out the responsibilities delegated to it by the U.S. Constitution or state law. In a few states, one board has responsibility for both public elementary and secondary education, and higher education. In other states, separate boards have these responsibilities. For publicly supported institutions, each state also has one or two departments that administer board policies and other regulations. The names of these departments are not uniform across the fifty states, but in all cases they are the arms of the state government entrusted with administration and management of the system of public schooling. That system includes public elementary and secondary education (kindergarten through twelfth grade), vocational education and special schools, and public higher education.

Governance and control of private K–12 schools, including charter schools, varies by state. In some states, private schools are monitored only for sanitation and safety; in others, curriculum, teacher competence, and other matters are regulated.

Elementary and Secondary Education

State departments of education are headed by a chief state school officer, called *superintendent of public instruction* in 27 cases, *commissioner of education* in 18, *secretary of education* in 3, and *director of education* in 2. The chief is elected by the people in 15 states, appointed by the state board of education in 26, and appointed by the governor in 9. Most chiefs are former public school or university educators. In most states the chief is required to be an educator.

The staffs of state departments of education have grown tremendously since the 1960s, partly because of federal contributions to states. Although only about 7 or 8 percent of state expenditures for education come from federal money, the federal outlay to states increased from $13 billion to more than $51 billion between 1980 and 2002. As a consequence, staff have been added to handle programs such as school improvement, education of people with disabilities, education of the disadvantaged, bilingual education, rehabilitation services, vocational and adult education, library services, and Indian education.

People in state education departments implement state policies and regulations in many areas, such as qualifications for teachers and administrators; basic education and other curricula; teacher education; selection of textbooks; and data collection on enrollments, attendance, transportation, and special needs. Programs in special education, compensatory education, vocational education and rehabilitation (not always a responsibility of the department of education), and adult education are substantial, each with some support from the federal government.

State staff provide technical assistance in all the areas just named. They also produce reports, conduct studies, convene and consult with school-teachers and administrators, and work with teacher educators in both public and private colleges and universities. They introduce and coordinate state initiatives in education. Among recent ones have been mentor teachers, standards for student achievement, reduction of violence in schools, reform in teacher education, AIDS prevention, and teacher evaluation. In earlier years, state education department staff were primarily data collectors and inspectors. More recently the trend has been toward provision of technical assistance and leadership to local districts.

State education department personnel spend much of their time administering federally funded programs. The paperwork required for certain federal programs is so time-consuming that many staff are, in effect, bound to their desks. Some think that this has brought about a neglect of state initiatives. State prerogatives in relation to federal programs have been increased since the advent of block grants to the states, which provide more discretion than the many categorical programs of yesteryear.

Preparation for professional jobs in state departments of education is basically that described in Chapters 2 through 5. That is, most state education department employees begin as public school teachers, and many then serve as public school administrators, supervisors, or specialists. A few have been employed in colleges of education. Most have at least a master's degree; many hold doctorates.

Employment is secured through application for announced openings, which must be made public to conform with affirmative action regulations. Despite the open system, some jobs may be *wired*—that is, the preferred choice may be in the wings waiting for the legal procedures to take their course. Getting to know state education department officials can be one of the key moves for access to notices of job openings and may be helpful in securing employment.

State education department jobs are part of civil service, except for the top few. Employees enjoy the standard benefits in salaries and fringe benefits provided for all state employees. There is typically a salary schedule. Where a person is placed on a salary schedule depends on level of training and experience. Some states advance personnel on the salary schedule only on merit; others grant salary increases annually (usually in eight to ten steps) unless there is a budget crisis or an employee has not been performing satisfactorily. Annual evaluations of performance by unit heads provide the evidence on which raises, merit jumps, or denial of raises is justified and authorized.

New York state's jobs provide an example of salary ranges. In 2003 the lowest-grade professional staff member started in the high $30,000s, and the highest-paid member earned $81,000 after a series of steps (on merit). In New York's top grade for professional administrative staff (for instance, division heads), the salary begins at $60,000 and rises to $130,000.

Civil service protects state employees from politically motivated harassment and discrimination. However, many veteran employees tell tales of administrations in which they (or colleagues) were essentially banned or rendered inoperative because of differences of opinion or style with the elected or appointed chief. Bureaucrats learn to survive the vicissitudes of different administrations. The staff member who concentrates on the basic educational issues of the state and faithfully carries out the goals of the state board and state superintendent can (and should) remain aloof from partisan politics. Despite gripes and criticisms by state staff, many more seem stimulated and challenged in their jobs than in former years. "There's a feeling that education is going somewhere," one perceptive leader reported.

Generalizations about state departments of education are difficult, despite the foregoing description, because states vary so much in size, population, and other characteristics. The more populous states, such as California, Connecticut, New York, and Pennsylvania, have several hundred full-time professional staff members, whereas states with smaller populations, such as New Hampshire, North Dakota, and Wyoming, have very few professional state agency employees. Another illustration of the diversity is the difference in the salaries of chief state school officers, which ranged in 2002 from $75,000 to $170,000. In twelve of the smaller states, chiefs earned less than $100,000. The spread reflects the differences in complexity and magnitude of the various state departments' responsibilities.

Higher Education

During the great expansion of public higher education in the 1950s, 1960s, and 1970s, forty-nine states (Wyoming being the exception) created one or more central commissions or boards (hereafter collectively called *boards*) to facilitate administration and governance of public colleges and universities. These boards either superseded the separate boards responsible for policy and direction of the various state-supported colleges and universities or were put in place to coordinate the policies and functions of those separate boards. In some states, universities were able to resist such consolidation. In others the "flagship" institution (usually the oldest and most prestigious state university) escaped, but other state-supported institutions did not.

The purpose of the state boards is to reduce unneeded duplication, to increase efficiency, and to allocate funds judiciously among public institutions of higher education. They also may have limited purview over private higher education. Some of the boards have direct trusteeship over state institutions. Others function largely to coordinate planning, research, data collection, and budget review; to represent the institutions to the governor, the legislature, and the public; and to promote communication among institutions.

The state boards of higher education also are charged with determining the tasks to be done in higher education and deciding which institutions should undertake the tasks. The early deliberations on these issues most often were undertaken with input from the administrative leadership and the faculty of the public colleges and universities—most of whom resisted their loss of autonomy. The conflict to be resolved was (and is) how much autonomy was essential for the operation of a healthy, dynamic institution and how much coordination was necessary for efficient, reasonable attention to higher education in a state.

Careers as staff members of coordinating boards have developed. People in these roles must be capable of planning a rational system of higher education in the state, allocating roles and functions among the individual institutions, and controlling the allocation of resources appropriated by the legislature.

The staffs of coordinating boards may be large or small, depending on the size of the state and the number of institutions. In California, for example, there are three governing agencies: the Board of Governors of the California Community Colleges, overseeing more than one hundred two-year institutions; the Board of Trustees of the California State University and Colleges, overseeing twenty-three four-year institutions (formerly state colleges); and the Regents of the University of California, overseeing nine universities. To coordinate the three agencies, there is a Coordinating Council for Higher Education, which has an advisory role relative to the agencies and the state officials.

The staffs of state coordinating bodies (sometimes called *general administration*) study the various aspects of education that are relevant to their types of institutions and to the policy-making and other functions of their board. They do long- and short-range planning and projections that anticipate and respond to enrollments, educational needs, budget requirements, legal mandates, federal initiatives and funding, and other matters identified by their board. Often there is a division of duties along the lines of academic affairs, communication (public affairs and lobbying), finance, planning, research (on institutional and substantive issues), and student services. Coordinating board staff also serve as clearinghouses and conduits.

Senior staff on coordinating boards have experience in higher education and have earned advanced degrees. They are appointed and hold office at the pleasure of their board, although some have academic rank in the institution from which they were promoted (provided that the institution is one of those being coordinated).

In North Carolina the salaries of the chancellors (the chief executive officers of the individual universities) of the sixteen campuses range from $150,000 to $255,000. At General Administration, salaries of professional staff range from $40,000 to $300,000, the latter being the salary of the president of the sixteen campuses.

FEDERAL EDUCATION AGENCIES

Several federal agencies administer programs in education. The Department of Education, the National Science Foundation, the National Endowment for the Arts, the National Endowment for the Humanities, the Department of Defense, the Department of State, and the Department of Labor are among the most prominent. The Department of Education is the focus in this chapter because it administers most of the programs that affect public schools and higher education, and because careers in other agencies parallel those described for the Department of Education.

The bureaucracy in Washington often is maligned, and that of the Department of Education is no exception. Advanced to department status in 1980 (from being the Office of Education within the Department of Health, Education, and Welfare), it has survived a number of political battles since that time. The Reagan administration wanted to abolish it but was not successful. Criticism from conservatives continues, and threats to the department's existence remain. With the current public concern about and interest in education, though, the department probably will survive and have significant prominence in the years to come.

The department is headed by the secretary of education. Below him or her are a deputy secretary and an undersecretary. At the next level are heads or chiefs of various offices, such as elementary and secondary education, higher education, and special education and rehabilitative services. The secretary, the deputy, and the undersecretary are political appointees, serving at the pleasure of the president.

A few political appointees and a number of career personnel (that is, regular department employees with long service) are selected to the Senior Executive Service (SES) of the department. SES members who are career personnel are protected by civil service; those who are political appointees are not. The remaining department staff are mostly civil servants. They have job security comparable to that of college and university professors with tenure. A few of them are political appointees and serve a specified term.

Staff duties are divided roughly into two broad areas: operations and program. The operations people attend to management, collection of information and statistics on education in the nation, planning and budget, and interagency affairs. Program personnel are (or should be) national authorities in their area. They have antennae out around the country to find out what is happening and what issues policy makers need to consider. They provide advice and assistance to policy makers. They oversee the programs that the government sponsors or the work for which it contracts. They represent the federal perspective to local projects and strive to obtain the largest return for the expenditure.

Staff do research and writing, prepare requests for proposals, review and evaluate proposals, design new efforts, and draft and modify regulations. They build and maintain networks with counterparts in state departments of education, universities, and national associations. They serve in a liaison capacity for the department in meetings around Washington and across the nation. Also, they receive visitors and respond to inquiries.

Preparation for department staff positions usually involves experience and an advanced degree, typically the doctorate. The department employs very few people who have just received their doctorates and have no experience. It seeks people who have credibility in the field.

Education bureaucrats have the same salary and grade levels as personnel in other government departments. Professional staff normally have General Service (GS) grades from 11 to 16. Salaries increase gradually in ten steps in each of the grades. As of early 2003, the beginning salary in GS-11 was $42,976, which increased in ten steps to $55,873. In a career a staff member can be advanced in GS grade when openings occur. The top nonadministrative professional grade was GS-15, in which the beginning salary was $85,140, the highest $110,682.

Middle-level management personnel (people at GS-13, GS-14, and GS-15) advance in salary on merit (based on annual performance evaluations).

An invaluable salary and retirement provision of federal employment is *indexing*. That is, federal salaries and pensions are adjusted periodically to reflect changes in the Consumer Price Index, which measures cost of living. Since the introduction of that provision, changes in the index always have meant increases.

COUNCILS AND ASSOCIATIONS

The state government departments and boards discussed in the preceding sections have legal authority over the schools, colleges, and universities under their purview, and the federal agencies administering programs in education have some legal authority in circumstances in which federal funding or legislation applies. Most of the councils and associations described in this section only influence education. The accrediting agencies do more than influence it, but mainly in the institutions that volunteer to be inspected. Influence by any agency, of course, can be strong, especially when the image of an institution is at stake. Salaries and fringe benefits for council and association staff tend to keep pace with or exceed those of federal departments. Most council and association offices are in the Washington, D.C., area. As a consequence, staff remuneration and benefits need to be competitive to attract professionals of high caliber.

State Activity

National associations and unions have state affiliates or units that work at influencing decisions and public policy in such areas of education as school and college curriculum, personnel, and administration. Most of these groups represent teachers, school administrators, or professors. Elementary and secondary public school teachers, numbering 3.1 million in 2001, are people in common circumstances. They coalesce easily, in all fifty states having organizations with full-time staffs. (Only six states have fewer than 10,000 teachers.) The 1.3 million full-time and the nearly 500,000 part-time college and university faculty are a diverse group. In states in which they are organized, they have joined with teacher groups. State affiliates and units of both the National Education Association and the American Federation of Teachers have higher education faculty in their membership. Administrators also are organized at the state level, and in several states they employ full-time staff. Few other professional education groups are so formally organized and staffed at the state level.

These organizations bring demands and standards to state boards of education, state departments of education, higher education coordinating boards, state legislatures, and other state agencies and organizations. Many state teacher organizations are well staffed, their professional personnel being on a par in training and experience with government and academic staff. In fact, some move back and forth among such positions. They deal with the same topics and issues that government staff handle (as well as internal organizational agendas), except that they perform in an advocacy role for their members. For example, government bureaucrats may plan budgets that ultimately determine salaries of school and college employees. Association staff study and compare salary figures across a state and the nation to make a case with a state board, coordinating council, or legislature designed to influence an increase in appropriations and hence a boost in salaries. Staff play similar roles in attempting to influence standards of teacher preparation and certification, high school graduation requirements, specifications for testing programs, college admission standards, and innumerable other matters of concern to their members.

Association staff also work to influence decisions on salaries and working conditions at the school district and college level. Collective bargaining is a prominent tactic, but there also is research and involvement in study and advisory committees. Association representatives appear before legislative committees, make presentations at state board hearings, and confer with governors. Collectively, associations are a political force. They lobby and participate in elections, not infrequently running one or more of their own members for political office. Teachers and professors now are as well represented as other businesspeople and professionals in some state legislatures.

State association staff are mostly former teachers and administrators. A few have been college professors. They have at least a bachelor's degree, more often a master's or higher degree. Usually they have experience as the kind of educator the association serves. That is, former teachers staff teacher organizations, and administrators become staff members of administrator associations. A frequent avenue to an association staff position is through appointed and elected leadership positions in the association. Many state teacher association staff have been chairpersons of committees, local and state officers, or state presidents. Salaries for state association staff are higher than the salaries paid to the professionals they represent but vary greatly from one state to another.

Regional and National Activity

One step above activities at the state level are those at the regional and national level. These include accrediting agencies, regional educational laboratories, research and development centers, regional technology in education consortia, clearinghouses, and national associations and councils.

Regional and National Accrediting Agencies

Accrediting at the regional and national levels is a voluntary method of quality control. Institutions apply to be reviewed. In addition to colleges and universities, high schools and (in some regions) elementary schools can be accredited by regional associations. Standards for accreditation are set by professionals in a particular field with the approval of the constituencies involved. The process involves a visit to the institution seeking accreditation by a team of professionals in the field or fields under examination. An institution must be visited periodically—say, every five years—to maintain its accredited standing. The institution is evaluated on the basis of standards that have been made known to it and that serve as criteria against which the team makes an assessment. Sometimes the institution prepares a report in advance. The report may be a self-study to inform the team how the institution measures up to criteria included in the accreditation body's standards.

The visiting team reports to a council or some other official body of the agency, and generally that body makes the decision on accreditation status. The usual actions are either approval, deferral, denial, probation, or suspension. These possibilities vary with the level of educational program being examined, the field (in higher education), and other considerations, such as whether an entire college is being reviewed or separate programs within a college. There is normally a fee for accreditation, and often the institution must pay the expenses of the visiting team. Regional accreditation, which is a review of an entire institution, usually takes the form of giving advice for needed improvement, particularly with institutions that have been accredited before. National accreditation (mainly in higher education) involves inspection of various professional programs and more often takes the approach of applying standards.

Six regional accrediting agencies—the Middle States, New England, North Central, Northwest, Southern, and Western associations of schools and colleges—accredit colleges and universities for general quality. They also accredit high schools and, in some states, elementary, middle, and junior high schools. Further, more than fifty national specialized accrediting organizations set standards and review professional programs of training in the major professions. Information on each one can be secured from the Council on Higher Education Accreditation.

Accrediting agencies do more than inspect whether the curriculum is adequate. They review such factors as institutional objectives, program quality, administrative effectiveness, financial stability, faculty and library strength, and adequacy of student personnel programs. The National Council for Accreditation of Teacher Education (NCATE) assesses the adequacy of curriculum design, delivery, and content; the strength of the program's relationship to the world of practice; the extent of diversity among students and the adequacy of procedures for monitoring, advising, and evaluating them; the quality and the size of faculty; and the adequacy of a program's governance and resources. Most important, it inquires into whether the performance of a program's graduate demonstrates acquisition of the knowledge, the skills, and the attitudes of a competent teacher.

The Teacher Education Accreditation Council (TEAC) requires faculty in programs seeking accreditation to affirm their commitment to preparing "competent, caring, and qualified educators." This affirmation must include evidence that faculty have an accurate and balanced understanding of the academic disciplines connected with their program—that is, subject matter knowledge, pedagogical knowledge, and teaching skill. In addition, faculty must present evidence that they have employed multiple measures and assessment methods to achieve dependable findings about a candidate's accomplishments. Finally, faculty must show that a system of inquiry, review, and quality control is in place to effect program improvement.

The illustrations suggest some of the tasks that NCATE and TEAC staff must accomplish. NCATE has several constituent organizations, representing various branches of the teaching profession. Staff are responsible for liaison with these organizations. They also manage the selection of visiting teams, arrange visitation schedules, receive reports and prepare them for presentation to the council, and carry out administrative work to support council meetings. They introduce new institutions to the standards of the council, conduct training sessions for members of visiting teams, and manage the evaluation of team members' performance. NCATE's standards are revised periodically. Staff have a part in the arrangements for, and the process of, revision.

TEAC staff have similar administrative tasks but also work to get their comparatively new accrediting agency under way. The style and the substance of accreditation is different in the two agencies. Basically, TEAC requires an institution to describe its goals and objectives within a general framework and then provide evidence that it is reaching those aspirations while using what it learns about its program to initiate continuous improvement. In contrast, NCATE evaluates an institution against standards that it has established with wide consultation in the teaching profession.

The staff members at the two accrediting agencies are few. The presidents and the other top staff hold doctorates and are experienced in teacher education. Most originally were teachers. They are selected by their councils through a search similar to the procedure followed by universities seeking deans. Second-line staff are appointed by the president of the council from applicants who respond to advertised openings. Salaries are in the $50,000 to $200,000 range. Professional employees are covered for retirement by the Teachers Insurance Annuity Association College Retirement Equities Fund (TIAA–CREF) and have other benefits similar to university faculty and national agencies and association employees.

Regional Educational Laboratories, Research and Development Centers, Regional Technology in Education Consortia, and Clearinghouses

201
Careers in Governance
and Control of Education

Ten regional educational laboratories, eight research and development (R&D) centers, ten Regional Technology in Education Consortia (RTECs), and sixteen Educational Resources Information Center (ERIC) clearinghouses are funded by the federal government. A list of the locations and the specific areas of investigation of these agencies is available from the U.S. Department of Education.

The laboratories focus on problems and issues in education and develop models and programs for implementation in the schools in their respective regions.

The R&D centers conduct research and development on particular topics, such as achievement in school mathematics and science, cultural diversity and second-language learning, and postsecondary improvement.

The RTEC program was established in 1995 to help states, school districts, adult literacy centers, and other education institutions use technology to support improved teaching and student learning. Attending to the needs of the various regions of the country, the ten consortia support professional development, technical assistance, and information dissemination. They work in a complementary and collaborative way with federally funded providers of technical assistance and with other nationwide educational technology support efforts. The ten consortia serve various geographical areas of the United States.

The ERIC clearinghouses index and abstract the educational literature. They also collect and store hard-to-find literature and make it available for retrieval. Each center specializes in a particular area of education. One specializes in teaching and teacher education.

Laboratory staff are mostly people who specialize in curriculum and instruction, including the subjects of the school curriculum. Many are expert in developing materials, running workshops, and consulting on school improvement. They come largely from public school and college ranks. Their training is typically in teacher education or a specialty field, with advanced study in a subject or an area of curriculum.

R&D staff include various types of researchers and a number of people with experience and expertise in policy development, curriculum development, and the specialty of a particular center. These staff are largely former college and university professors. Many have held positions in public schools.

Most professional staff of the laboratories and the R&D centers hold doctorates and have had considerable work experience. Jobs in the laboratories and the centers are secured by application for advertised positions. Most R&D centers are operated by universities on contract with the federal government. Hence, several staff are tenured university professors with a part- or full-time assignment to the center. Professionals hired by an R&D center who have no formal ties to the contracting university may not have job security beyond the term of federal support.

In the RTECs the senior professional staff members typically hold doctorates, the junior members master's degrees.

The professional education staffs of ERIC clearinghouses are typically small. Often the director and other top staff are trained in the field in which the clearinghouse specializes.

National Associations and Councils

Thousands of professional educators staff the hundreds of associations and councils at the national level. Most of these groups are located in and around the nation's capital (see the Appendix for addresses). The access to federal agencies and Congress and the proximity to related education associations make metropolitan Washington a convenient location.

Describing the roles and the functions of all the education associations and councils operating at the national level is too extensive an undertaking for this book. Details about their membership, function, role, and activities can be found on the Internet (see the Appendix for their website addresses) and in the *Encyclopedia of Associations*.

National associations and councils fall into several categories, according to their unit of membership. The best known are those that offer membership to individuals, and the largest of them are teacher organizations. The two most prominent ones, the National Education Association and the American Federation of Teachers, are for teachers generally, regardless of level or subject. Other teacher groups (to which a number of college professors also belong) are subject matter associations focused on the various subjects taught in schools, such as the National Council for the Social Studies, the National Council of Teachers of English, and the National Council of Teachers of Mathematics.

There are general membership groups for college teachers as well. The American Association of University Professors and the American Association of University Women are examples. Further, college teachers participate in subject matter groups, such as the American Chemical Society, the American Political Science Association, the American Psychological Association, the American Sociological Association, and the Association of American Geographers. These organizations are more broadly based than the subject matter associations for teachers, drawing members from all personnel educated in the subject above a certain level. So, for example, the American Chemical Society serves not only professors of chemistry but also chemists in business and industry.

There also are associations for personnel in public schools and higher education whose jobs are alike. Some examples are the American Association of Collegiate Registrars and Admissions Officers, the American Association of School Personnel Administrators, the American Association of University Administrators, the Association for Supervision and Curriculum Development, the National Association of College and University Business Officers, and the National Association of Elementary School Principals.

In a second category are associations whose unit of membership is an institution. There are two kinds of these: associations in which an entire institution is a member, such as the National Association of State Universities and Land-Grant Colleges, the American Association of State Colleges and Universities, and the Association of American Universities; and those to which professional schools belong, such as the American Association of Colleges for Teacher Education, the Association of American Law Schools, the Association of Collegiate Schools of Architecture, and the Association of Schools of Public Health.

Still another category of organizations is councils that have associations as members. The Council on Higher Education Accreditation, for example, counts accrediting associations among its members.

Such organizations are typically staffed predominantly by people who were once the type of professional served by the organization or who have come from the institutions that the organization serves. The essential background for these positions usually includes experience in the specialty of the organization. In the teacher associations, almost all have been teachers. They may or may not have earned doctorates, but most have a master's degree. In the higher education associations, the common academic credential required of professional staff is the doctorate.

Although the tasks that association staff perform vary, some activities are common to most association personnel. They listen, observe, think, and talk—absorbing, reflecting, evaluating, contributing. They write—memos, newsletters, proposals, reports, monographs, letters, and more. They read continuously—research reports; newsletters, journals, and newspapers in their field; policy and position papers; proposed legislation; and government regulations. Speaking and writing and getting along with people are important skills. The flow of information across a staff member's desk is constant and voluminous. Selecting what to read is an everyday task.

Most association staff attend meetings within and outside their organization. They spend much time on the telephone and with E-mail answering queries, promoting the program and the position of their organization, maintaining a network of contacts, learning about developments, and making arrangements.

Many staff travel extensively—speaking, attending meetings, visiting institutions, conducting workshops and conferences, representing the organization, advising, and consulting.

Larger associations specialize the work of their staff. Some common categories are membership, publications, conferences and meetings, government relations, public relations, research, educational affairs, professional affairs, scientific affairs, and continuing education. These divisions are peculiar to individual and institutional membership organizations and are not as valid for accrediting agencies.

A number of associations administer voluntary programs that examine and *credential* (professionally certify) practitioners in their field. Candidates must usually be members of the association. Such programs are a profession's own effort to ensure high standards of competence on the part of its members. Some of the bodies that apply these standards have been legally sanctioned by state legislatures. Others issue credentials in addition to, or instead of, state certification or licensure.

Many national associations in education participate in the National Board for Professional Teaching Standards, a comparatively new organization designed to attest to the competence of public school teachers at an advanced level—comparable to the diplomate in other fields. Teachers must apply and qualify for this national certification.

Salaries and fringe benefits in metropolitan Washington compete with those of government employees. Many organizations miss that mark. Some exceed it.

The National Education Association provides an example of association salaries. The range for its professional staff is $34,664 to $113,273; for its managerial staff, $60,565 to $127,247.

Fringe benefits are generally comparable. They include hospitalization and medical insurance, retirement programs (with higher education associations offering TIAA–CREF), life insurance, and a liberal leave policy (usually the equivalent of a month's annual leave and all legal holidays). Vision and dental care insurance are offered by more and more agencies.

ROOM AT THE TOP

Many of the staff positions described in this chapter are second or third careers for people in education. They come well after graduation from college, after successful experience and graduate study.

Moreover, once a person secures a government, association, or council job, education continues. Every week and year at work is a learning experience. Many people in these positions take advanced graduate work and complete a doctorate or some other degree in part-time study as their careers move along. There are both personal and professional benefits in such continuing education.

As in any field, people in the top jobs, often the more experienced, gradually grow older and retire. The lieutenants know the content and the procedures of the job; they understand the function and the purpose of the organization; they have built networks with constituents. They often are the heirs apparent. There is room at the top.

FIRSTHAND ACCOUNT

Allen Schmieder earned a B.S. in education at Edinboro University of Pennsylvania with majors in English and geography, and a master's and Ph.D. in geography at The Ohio State University (OSU). After teaching geography for ten years, first at OSU and then at the University of Maryland (UM),

Dr. Schmieder joined the U.S. Office of Education (USOE), now the Department of Education (DOE), where he served for thirty-two years. He is currently vice president for K–20 education at JDL Technologies in Minnesota. He describes how he gained entry to government employment and offers advice to those with similar career goals.

During my tenure at OSU, I became increasingly unhappy with the low priority given to education and education students. I wanted to elevate teacher education to the highest possible level of importance. I moved to the Washington, DC, area and took a job at UM so that I could study the federal government and become a part of it. I became a field reader of grant proposals for USOE and the National Science Foundation. I also actively sought help from savvy colleagues in several educational associations. Further, I wrote a proposal to USOE seeking funding for a summer institute for junior high school geography teachers. The application was ranked second of 120, catching the attention of USOE and leaders in my professional association. As a result, I was asked to join USOE to lead the geography institutes program.

I rose through the ranks, becoming head of all social sciences and, as a result of that experience, leader of eight field task forces on educational change. These task forces identified competency-based education and teacher centers, among other educational trends, as two critical levers for education reform. Using the power and resources of national education groups, my colleagues and I launched major national initiatives in these two areas.

Later a new administration killed these programs (a storm to be weathered many times by anyone choosing a government career), and I was placed on the shelf in the hope that I would become discouraged and leave the government. I worked diligently to determine what I could do that needed to be done and would make me indispensable to the new administration. I did not want to abandon my determination to be in a national position to help teachers. I befriended people at the major technology companies and with their help set up DOE's first voluntary technology training center. The center impressed the new policy players sufficiently that I was drawn into their circles.

Shortly afterward, I was asked to head Title II of the Education for Economic Security Act, which eventually became the Eisenhower National Program for Mathematics, Science, Technology, and Foreign Languages. Remembering the successful elements of my earlier years, I formed a national steering committee of powerful educational leaders from the ten DOE regions and representatives from major federal agencies. The program was highly successful and eventually generated the Eisenhower National Clearinghouse and Regional Eisenhower Consortiums.

Eventually I locked horns with a DOE administrator (a businessman), and I was moved to the core-subjects standards programs. Gradually, probably because of my experience in policy-level administration, I took over several additional programs, including Computer Assisted Instruction, Technology Education, and the Fund for Educational Innovation.

When the White House launched the GLOBE Program, I was detailed to the Office of the Vice President to become the deputy director for education. After completing that three-year assignment, I returned to DOE to become a program director for the Technology Innovation Challenge Grants and the technology director of the Blue Ribbon Schools Program. I retired in 1998 for personal reasons.

Advice

Government service is a high calling and needs a broad range of bright and ambitious people. Almost every government agency includes people doing the work of education, so don't limit your sights to agencies that do only education. After DOE, the departments with the largest education budgets are Agriculture, Defense, and Health and Human Services.

Study the websites of all the major federal departments, and list the programs you want to be related to. Those websites include directions for making application for employment. Visit Washington. Most agencies have a bulletin board on which jobs are advertised. Spend several days visiting agencies with potential work for you. You may meet someone who will take a liking to you and help you find a job. It is easier to get your foot in an open door and then move laterally within an agency or between agencies than to push through a door that is not likely to open. In some cases, support from your local congressional representatives can help. An even more successful approach is to identify an official already in the government who knows your qualifications and seek his or her help in gaining entry. Be persistent. Go for it!

APPENDIX

DIRECTORY OF
EDUCATION
ORGANIZATIONS

American Alliance for Health,
   Physical Education, Recreation
   and Dance (AAHPERD)
1900 Association Drive
Reston, VA 20191
aahperd.org

American Association for Adult
   and Continuing Education
   (AAACE)
4380 Forbes Boulevard
Lanham, MD 20706
aaace.org

American Association for
   Employment in Education
   (AAEE)
3040 Riverside Drive, Suite 125
Columbus, OH 43221-2550
aaee.org

American Association for Health
   Education (AAHE)
1900 Association Drive
Reston, VA 20191-1598
aahperd.org/aahe

American Association for Higher
   Education (AAHE)
One Dupont Circle, Suite 360
Washington, DC 20036
aahe.org

American Association of
   Christian Schools (AACS)
P.O. Box 1097
Independence, MO 64051-0597
aacs.org

American Association of Colleges
for Teacher Education (AACTE)
1307 New York Avenue NW, Suite
300
Washington, DC 20005
aacte.org

American Association of
Collegiate Registrars and
Admissions Officers (AACRAO)
One Dupont Circle NW, Suite 520
Washington, DC 20036
aacrao.org

American Association of
Community Colleges (AACC)
One Dupont Circle NW, Suite 410
Washington, DC 20036
aacc.nche.edu

American Association of Family
and Consumer Sciences
(AAFCS)
1555 King Street
Alexandria, VA 22314
aafcs.org

American Association of Physics
Teachers (AAPT)
One Physics Ellipse
College Park, MD 20740-3845
aapt.org

American Association of School
Administrators (AASA)
801 North Quincy Street, Suite 700
Arlington, VA 22203-1730
aasa.org

American Association of School
Personnel Administrators
(AASPA)
3080 Brickhouse Court
Virginia Beach, VA 23452
aaspa.org

American Association of State
Colleges and Universities
(AASCU)
1307 New York Avenue NW, Fifth
Floor
Washington, DC 20005-1701
aascu.org

American Association of Teachers
of Spanish and Portuguese
(AATSP)
423 Exton Commons
Exton, PA 19341-2451
aatsp.org

American Association of
University Administrators
(AAUA)
P.O. Box 261363
Plano, TX 75026-1363
http://aaua.org

American Association of
University Professors
(AAUP)
1012 Fourteenth Street NW,
Suite 500
Washington, DC 20005
aaup.org

American Association of
University Women
(AAUW)
1111 Sixteenth Street NW
Washington, DC 20036
aauw.org

American College Personnel
Association (ACPA)
One Dupont Circle, Suite 300
Washington, DC 20036
acpa.nche.edu

American Council of Learned
Societies (ACLS)
633 Third Avenue
New York, NY 10017-6795
acls.org

American Council on Education
(ACE)
One Dupont Circle NW, Suite 800
Washington, DC 20036
acenet.edu

American Council on the
Teaching of Foreign Languages
(ACTFL)
Six Executive Plaza
Yonkers, NY 10701-6801
actfl.org

American Counseling Association
(ACA)
5999 Stevenson Avenue
Alexandria, VA 22304-3300
counseling.org

American Driver and Traffic
Safety Education Association
(ADTSEA)
Highway Safety Center
Indiana University of Pennsylvania
Indiana, PA 15705
adtsea.iup.edu/adtsea

American Educational Research
Association (AERA)
1230 Seventeenth Street NW
Washington, DC 20036
aera.net

American Federation of Teachers
(AFT)
555 New Jersey Avenue NW
Washington, DC 20001
aft.org

American Library Association
(ALA)
50 East Huron Street
Chicago, IL 60611
ala.org

American Nurses Association
(ANA)
600 Maryland Avenue SW, Suite
100 West
Washington, DC 20024
ana.org

American Occupational Therapy
Association (AOTA)
4720 Montgomery Lane
Bethesda, MD 20824-1220
aota.org

American Physical Therapy
Association (APTA)
1111 North Fairfax Street
Alexandria, VA 22314
apta.org

American Psychological
Association (APA)
750 First Street NE
Washington, DC 20002
apa.org

American School Counselor
Association (ASCA)
801 North Fairfax Street,
Suite 310
Alexandria, VA 22314
schoolcounselor.org

American School Health
Association (ASHA)
7263 State Route 43
Kent, OH 44240
ashaweb.org

American Society for
Training
and Development (ASTD)
1640 King Street, Box 1443
Alexandria, VA 22313-2043
astd.org

American Speech-Language-
Hearing Association (ASHA)
10801 Rockville Pike
Rockville, MD 20852
asha.org

Association for Career and
Technical Education
(ACTE)
1410 King Street
Alexandria, VA 22314
acteonline.org

Association for Childhood
Education International
(ACEI)
17904 Georgia Avenue,
Suite 215
Olney, MD 20832
udel.edu/bateman/acei

Association for Educational
Communications and
Technology (AECT)
1800 North Stonelake Drive,
Suite 2
Bloomington, IN 47408
aect.org

Association for Institutional
Research (AIR)
Florida State University
222 Stone Building
Tallahassee, FL 32306-4462
http://airweb.org

Association for Supervision and
Curriculum Development
(ASCD)
1703 Beauregard Street
Alexandria, VA 22311-1714
ascd.org

Association for the Study of
Higher Education (ASHE)
University of Missouri–Columbia
202 Hill Hall
Columbia, MO 65211-2190
ashe.missouri.edu

Association of American Colleges
and Universities (AAC&U)
1818 R Street NW
Washington, DC 20009
aacu.org

Association of American
Universities (AAU)
1200 New York Avenue NW, Suite
550
Washington, DC 20005
aau.edu

Association of Canadian
Community Colleges (ACCC)
200-1223 rue Michael Street N
Ottawa, Ontario, Canada K1J 7T2
accc.ca

Association of Christian Schools
International (ACSI)
731 Chapel Hills Drive
Colorado Springs, CO 80920
www.acsi.org

Association of Information
Technology Professionals (AITP)
401 North Michigan Avenue, Suite
2200
Chicago, IL 60611-4267
aitp.org

Association of School Business
Officials, International (ASBO)
11401 North Shore Drive
Reston, VA 22090-4232
asbointl.org

Association of Teacher Educators
(ATE)
1900 Association Drive
Reston, VA 20191
atel.org

Association of Universities and
Colleges of Canada (AUCC)
350 Albert Street, Suite 600
Ottawa, Ontario, Canada K1R 1B1
aucc.ca

Canadian Association of College
and University Student Services
(CACUSS)
University of Toronto
214 College Street, Room 307
Toronto, Ontario, Canada M5T 2Z9
cacuss.ca

Canadian Association of
University Teachers (CAUT)
2675 Queensview Drive
Ottawa, Ontario, Canada K2B 8K2
caut.ca

Canadian Teachers' Federation
(CTF)
2490 Don Reid Drive
Ottawa, Ontario, Canada K1H 1E1
ctf-fce.ca

Carnegie Foundation for the
Advancement of Teaching
555 Middlefield Road
Menlo Park, CA 94025-3443
carnegiefoundation.org/index2
.htm

Center of Education for the Young
Adolescent (CEYA)
University of
Wisconsin–Platteville
134 Doudna Hall, 1 University
Plaza
Platteville, WI 53818-3099
uwplatt.edu/~ceya

College and University
Professional Association for
Human Resources
(CUPA–HR)
Tyson Place
2607 Kingston Pike, Suite 250
Knoxville, TN 37919
cupahr.org

Council for American Private
Education (CAPE)
13017 Wisteria Drive, PMB 457
Germantown, MD 20874
capenet.org

Council for Basic Education
(CBE)
1319 F Street NW, Suite 900
Washington, DC 20004
c-b-e.org

Council for Exceptional Children
(CEC)
1110 North Glebe Road, Suite 300
Arlington, VA 22201-5704
cec.sped.org

Council for Higher Education
Accreditation (CHEA)
One Dupont Circle NW, Suite 510
Washington, DC 20036-1135
chea.org

Council on Social Work Education
(CSWE)
1725 Duke Street, Suite 500
Alexandria, VA 22314
cswe.org

Council for Advancement and
Support of Education (CASE)
1307 New York Avenue NW, Suite
1000
Washington, DC 20005-4701
case.org

Council of Chief State School
Officers (CCSSO)
One Massachusetts Avenue NW,
Suite 700
Washington, DC 20001-1431
ccsso.org

Council of Graduate Schools
(CGS)
One Dupont Circle NW, Suite 430
Washington, DC 20036
cgsnet.org

Council on Technology Teacher Education (CTTE)
Illinois State University
211A Turner Hall, Campus Box 5100
Normal, IL 61790
teched.vt.edu/ctte

Defense Activity for Non-Traditional Education Support (DANTES)
6490 Saufley Field Road
Pensacola, FL 32509-5243
www.dantes.doded.mil

Distance Education and Training Council (DETC)
1601 18th Street NW
Washington, DC 20009
detc.org

Education Commission of the States (ECS)
700 Broadway, Suite 1200
Denver, CO 80203
ecs.org

Educational Research Service (ERS)
2000 Clarendon Boulevard
Arlington, VA 22201
ers.org

ERIC Clearinghouse on Higher Education
George Washington University
Graduate School of Education and Human Development
One Dupont Circle NW, Suite 630
Washington, DC 20036-1183
eriche.org

ERIC Clearinghouse on Teaching and Teacher Education
1307 New York Avenue NW, Suite 300
Washington, DC 20005-4701
ericsp.org

Graduate School, USDA
U.S. Department of Agriculture
600 Maryland Avenue SW
Washington, DC 20024
http://grad.usda.gov

Institute of Education Sciences
U.S. Department of Education
555 New Jersey Avenue NW
Washington, DC 20208
ed.gov/offices/IES

Institute of International Education (IIE)
809 United Nations Plaza
New York, NY 10017-3580
www.iie.org

International Reading Association
(IRA)
800 Barksdale Road
P.O. Box 8139
Newark, DE 19714-8139
reading.org

International Society for
Technology in Education (ISTE)
480 Charnelton Street
Eugene, OR 97401-2626
iste.org

International Technology
Education Association (ITEA)
1914 Association Drive
Reston, VA 20191
iteawww.org

John Dewey Society
Educational Leadership and
Professional Studies
State University of West Georgia
1600 Maple Street
Carrolton, GA 30118

Modern Language Association
(MLA)
26 Broadway, Third Floor
New York, NY 10004-1789
www.mla.org

MENC: The National Association
for Music Education
1806 Robert Fulton Drive
Reston, VA 20191
menc.org

National Academy of Sciences
500 Fifth Street NW
Washington, DC 20001
www.nas.edu

National Art Education
Association (NAEA)
1916 Association Drive
Reston, VA 20191
naea-reston.org

National Association for Family
and Community Education
(NAFCE)
73 Cavalier Boulevard, Suite 106
Florence, KY 41042
nafce.org

National Association for Gifted
Children (NAGC)
1707 L Street NW, Suite 550
Washington, DC 20036
nagc.org

National Association of
Independent Colleges and
Universities (NAICU)
1025 Connecticut Avenue NW,
Suite 700
Washington, DC 20036
naicu.edu

National Association for the
Education of Young Children
(NAEYC)
1509 16th Street NW
Washington, DC 20036
naeyc.org

National Association of Federal
    Education Program
    Administrators (NAFEPA)
c/o John Pfaff, President
830 Virginia Avenue
Sheboygan, WI 53081
nafepa.org

National Association of Biology
    Teachers (NABT)
12030 Sunrise Valley Drive, Suite
    110
Reston, VA 20191
nabt.org

National Association of
    Elementary School Principals
    (NAESP)
1615 Duke Street
Alexandria, VA 22314
naesp.org

National Association of
    Independent Colleges and
    Universities (NAICU)
1025 Connecticut Avenue NW,
    Suite 700
Washington, DC 20036
naicu.edu

National Association of
    Independent Schools (NAIS)
1620 L Street NW, Suite 1100
Washington, DC 20036-5695
nais.org

National Association of Student
    Personnel Administrators
    (NASPA)
1875 Connecticut Avenue NW,
    Suite 418
Washington, DC 20009
naspa.org

National Association of School
    Nurses (NASN)
P.O. Box 1300
Scarborough, ME 04070-1300
nasn.org

National Association of School
    Psychologists (NASP)
4340 East West Highway, Suite 402
Bethesda, MD 20814-4411
nasponline.org

National Association of Schools of
    Art and Design (NASAD)
11250 Roger Bacon Drive, Suite 21
Reston, VA 20190
arts-accredit.org/nasad

National Association of Schools of
    Music (NASM)
11250 Roger Bacon Drive, Suite 21
Reston, VA 20190
arts-accredit.org/nasm/nasm.htm

National Association of Schools of
    Theatre (NAST)
11250 Roger Bacon Drive, Suite 21
Reston, VA 20190
arts-accredit.org/nast

National Association of Secondary
School Principals (NASSP)
1904 Association Drive
Reston, VA 20191
nassp.org

National Association of Social
Workers (NASW)
750 First Street NE, Suite 700
Washington, DC 20002-4241
socialworkers.org

National Association of State
Directors of Special Education
(NASDSE)
1800 Diagonal Road, Suite 320
Alexandria, VA 22314
nasdse.org

National Association of State
Directors of Teacher Education
and Certification (NASDTEC)
39 Nathan Ellis Highway, PMB
#134
Mashpee, MA 02649-3267
nasdtec.org

National Association of State
Directors of Career Technical
Education Consortium
(NASDCTEC)
444 North Capitol Street NW,
Suite 830
Washington, DC 20001
careertech.org

National Association of State
Universities and Land-Grant
Colleges (NASULGC)
1307 New York Avenue NW
Washington, DC 20005
nasulgc.org

National Association of Student
Financial Aid Administrators
(NASFAA)
1129 20th Street NW, Suite 400
Washington, DC 20036-3453
nasfaa.org

National Association of University
Women (NAUW)
1001 E Street SE
Washington, DC 20003
nauw.org

National Association for Year-
Round Education (NAYRE)
P.O. Box 711386
San Diego, CA 92171
nayre.org

National Board for Professional
Teaching Standards (NBPTS)
1525 Wilson Boulevard, Suite 500
Arlington, VA 22209
nbpts.org

National Business Education
Association (NBEA)
1914 Association Drive
Reston, VA 20191
nbea.org

National Catholic Educational
Association (NCEA)
1077 30th Street NW, Suite 100
Washington, DC 20007-3852
ncea.org

National Center for Education
Statistics (NCES)
U.S. Department of Education
1990 K Street NW
Washington, DC 20006
nces.ed.gov

National Clearinghouse for
Professions in Special
Education
The Council for Exceptional
Education
1110 North Glebe Road,
Suite 300
Arlington, VA 22201-5704
special-ed-careers.org

National Community Education
Association (NCEA)
3929 Old Lee Highway,
Suite 91-A
Fairfax, VA 22030
ncea.com

National PTA
330 North Wabash Avenue, Suite
2100
Chicago, IL 60611-3690
pta.org

National Council for Accreditation
of Teacher Education (NCATE)
2010 Massachusetts Avenue NW,
Suite 500
Washington, DC 20036-1023
ncate.org

National Council for Geographic
Education (NCGE)
Jacksonville State University
206A Martin Hall
Jacksonville, AL 36265-1602
ncge.org

National Council for History
Education (NCHE)
26915 Westwood Road, Suite B-2
Westlake, OH 44145-4657
history.org/nche

National Council for the Social
Studies (NCSS)
855 Sixteenth Street
Silver Spring, MD 20910
ncss.org

National Council of Teachers of
English (NCTE)
1111 Kenyon Road
Urbana, IL 61801-1096
ncte.org

National Council of Teachers of
Mathematics (NCTM)
1906 Association Drive
Reston, VA 20191-1502
nctm.org

National Education Association
(NEA)
Teaching and Learning
1201 16th Street NW
Washington, DC 20036-3290
nea.org

National Head Start Association
(NHSA)
1651 Prince Street
Alexandria, VA 22314
nhsa.org

National Information Center for
Children and Youth with
Disabilities (NICCYD)
P.O. Box 1492
Washington, DC 20013-1492
nichcy.org

National Middle School
Association (NMSA)
4151 Executive Parkway, Suite 300
Westerville, OH 43081
nmsa.org

National School Boards
Association (NSBA)
1680 Duke Street
Alexandria, VA 22314
nsba.org

National School Public Relations
Association (NSPRA)
15948 Derwood Road
Rockville, MD 20855-2123
nspra.org

National Science Foundation
(NSF)
4201 Wilson Boulevard
Arlington, VA 22230
nsf.gov

National Science Teachers
Association (NSTA)
1840 Wilson Boulevard
Arlington, VA 22201
nsta.org

National Society for Experiential
Education (NSEE)
9001 Braddock Road, Suite 380
Springfield, VA 22151
nsee.org

National Staff Development
Council (NSDC)
P.O. Box 240
Oxford, OH 45056
nsdc.org

National Training Laboratories
(NTL)
Institute for Applied Behavioral
Science
300 North Lee Street, Suite 300
Alexandria, VA 22314-2630
ntl.org

Public Broadcasting System, Adult
Learning Service
1320 Braddock Place
Alexandria, VA 22314
pbs.org/als

Recruiting New Teachers, Inc. (RNT)
385 Concord Avenue, Suite 103
Belmont, MA 02478
www.rnt.org

School Social Work Association of America (SSWAA)
P.O. Box 2072
Northlake, IL 60164
sswaa.org

Teacher Education Accreditation Council (TEAC)
One Dupont Circle, Suite 320
Washington, DC 20036-0110
teac.org

Teachers Insurance and Annuity Association College Retirement Equities Fund (TIAA–CREF)
730 Third Avenue
New York, NY 10017-3206
tiaa.org

Teachers of English to Speakers of Other Languages (TESOL)
700 South Washington Street, Suite 200
Alexandria, VA 22314-4287
tesol.org

United States Department of Education (USDOE)
400 Maryland Avenue SW
Washington, DC 20202-0498
Education Resource Organizations Directory
ed.gov/Programs/EROD

University Continuing Education Association (UCEA)
One Dupont Circle NW, Suite 615
Washington, DC 20036
ucea.edu

BIBLIOGRAPHY

GENERAL RESOURCES

Carnegie Forum on Education and the Economy. 1986. *A notion prepared: teachers for the 21st century*. The Report of the Task Force on Teaching as a Profession. New York: Author.

Educational rankings annual. Updated annually. Detroit, MI: Gale Research Co.

Educational Research Service. 1995. *Fringe benefits for superintendents in public schools, 1994–95*, Part 1 of *National survey of fringe benefits in public schools*. Arlington, VA: Author.

Educational Research Service. 2002. *Measuring changes in salaries and wages in public schools, 2002*. Arlington, VA: Author.

Educational Research Service. 2002. *Salaries for administrators and supervisors in public schools, 2001–2002*. Arlington, VA: Author.

Educational Research Service. 2002. *Salaries paid professional personnel in public schools, 2001–2002*, Part 2 of *National survey of salaries and wages in public schools*. Arlington, VA: Author.

Education Week. Weekly. Bethesda, MD: Editorial Projects in Education.

Gerald, D. E., and W. J. Hussar, eds. 2001. *Projections of education statistics to 2011*. Washington, DC: National Center for Education Statistics.

Gerald, D. E., and W. J. Hussar, eds. 2002. *Projections of education statistics to 2012*. Washington, DC: National Center for Education Statistics.

Goodlad, J. I. 1984. *A place called school: Prospects for the future.* New York: McGraw-Hill.

———. 1990. *Teachers for our nation's schools.* San Francisco: Jossey-Bass.

National Association of State Directors of Teacher Education and Certification. Updated annually. *The NASDTEC manual on preparation and certification of educational personnel.* Dubuque, IA: Kendall/Hunt.

National Center for Education Statistics. 2002. *Schools and staffing in the United States: A statistical profile.* Washington, DC: Author.

National Commission on Teaching & America's Future. 1996. *What matters most: Teaching for America's future.* New York: Author.

National Commission on Teaching & America's Future. 2003 (January). *No dream denied: A pledge to America's children.* New York: Author.

Occupational outlook handbook. Updated annually. Washington, DC: U.S. Government Printing Office. 2002–03 edition available online at www.bls.gov/oco/home.htm (last visited February 22, 2003).

Requirements for certification of teachers, counselors, librarians, administrators for elementary and secondary schools. Updated annually. Chicago: University of Chicago Press.

Rose, L. C., and A. M. Gallup, 2002. "The 34th annual Phi Delta Kappa/Gallup poll of the public's attitudes toward the public schools." *Phi Delta Kappan,* 84(1), 41–46, 51–56.

Sherman, J. D., E. Rowe, L. Peternick, and F. Johnson. 2002. *Financing elementary and secondary education in the states: 1997–98.* Research and Development Report. Washington, DC: National Center for Education Statistics.

U.S. Bureau of the Census. 2000. *Statistical abstract of the United States 2000,* 120th ed. Washington, DC: Hoover Business Press.

U.S. Department of Education. 2002. *Distance education instruction by postsecondary faculty and staff: Fall 1998.* Washington, DC: U.S. Government Printing Office.

Wirt, J., S. Choy, D. Gerald, S. Provasnik, P. Rooney, S. Watanabe, R. Tobin, M. Glander, B. Kridl, and A. Livingston. 2001. *The condition of education 2001.* Washington, DC: National Center for Education Statistics.

Wirt, J., S. Choy, D. Gerald, S. Provasnik, P. Rooney, S. Watanabe, R. Tobin, B. Kridl, and A. Livingston. 2002. *The condition of education 2002.* Washington, DC: National Center for Education Statistics.

World Economic Forum. 2003. *Global competitiveness report 2001–2002: Competitiveness file.* Available at www.weforum.org/site/homepublic .nsf/Content/Global+Competitiveness+Programme%5CReports%5CG lobal+Competitiveness+Report+2001-2002 (last visited February 27, 2003).

TEACHING IN K–12 SCHOOLS

American Association for Employment in Education. 2002. *Educator supply and demand in the United States: 2001 research report.* Columbus, OH: Author.

American Council on the Teaching of Foreign Languages, Foreign Language Teacher Standards Writing Team. 2002 (August). *Program standards for the preparation of foreign language teachers initial level—undergraduate and graduate for K–12 and secondary certification programs.* Yonkers, NY: Author. Available at www.ncate.org/standard/new%20program%20 standards/actfl2002.pdf (last visited February 27, 2003).

Association for Childhood Education International. 1998. *ACEI position paper: Preparation of early childhood education teachers.* Olney, MD: Author. Available at www.udel.edu/bateman/acei/prepec.htm (last visited February 27, 2003).

Association for Childhood Education International. 2002. *ACEI position paper: Preparation of elementary teachers.* Olney, MD: Author. Available at www.udel.edu/bateman/acei/prepel.htm (last visited February 27, 2003).

Bussis, A. M., E. A. Chittenden, and M. Amarel. 1976. *Beyond surface curriculum.* Boulder, CO: Westview Press.

Carnegie Forum on Education and the Economy. 1986. *A nation prepared: Teachers for the 21st century.* New York: Author.

Corwin, R. G., and R. A. Edelfelt, eds. 1977. *Perspectives on organizations: The school as a social organization.* Washington, DC: American Association of Colleges for Teacher Education & Association of Teacher Educators.

Council of Chief State School Officers. 1992. *Interstate New Teacher Assessment and Support Consortium standards.* Washington, DC: Author.

Edelfelt, R., and J. Raths. 1999. *A brief history of standards in teacher education.* Reston, VA: Association of Teacher Educators.

Haberman, M. 1995. *Star teachers of children in poverty.* West Lafayette, IN: Kappa Delta Pi.

Ingersoll, R. 2001. "Teacher turnover and teacher shortages: An organizational analysis." *American Education Research Journal*, 38, 499–534.

Kaplan, L., and R. A. Edelfelt, eds. 1996. *Teachers for the new millennium: Aligning teacher development, national goals, and high standards for all students.* Thousand Oaks, CA: Corwin Press.

McEwin, C. K., T. S. Dickinson, and D. Jenkins. 1996. *America's middle schools: Practices and progress. A 25-year perspective.* Columbus, OH: National Middle School Association.

MetLife Survey of the American Teacher. Conducted annually on a different topic. Available at www.metlife.com/Applications/Corporate/WPS/ CDA/PageGenerator/0,1674,P2315,00.html (last visited February 26, 2003).

Milner, J. O., R. Edelfelt, and P. T. Wilbur. 2001. *Developing teachers: Fifth year programs for outstanding students.* Lanham, MD: University Press of America.

National Association for the Education of Young Children. 2001. *NAEYC standards for early childhood professional preparation: Baccalaureate or initial licensure level.* Washington, DC: Author. Available at www.ncate. org/standard/new%20program%20standards/naeyc%202001.pdf (last visited February 27, 2003).

National Association for the Education of Young Children. 2002. *Career encounters.* (Video.) Washington, DC: Author.

National Association for the Education of Young Children. 2002. *Careers in early childhood education.* Washington, DC: Author.

National Center for Education Statistics. 1994. *Characteristics of stayers, movers, and leavers: Results from the teacher follow-up survey, 1991–92.* Washington, DC: Author.

National Center for Education Statistics. 2001. *Characteristics of the 100 largest public elementary and secondary school districts in the United States: 1999–2000.* Washington, DC: Author.

National Center for Education Statistics. 2002. *Schools and staffing in the United States: A statistical profile.* Washington, DC: Author.

National Council for Accreditation of Teacher Education. 2000. *Program standards for elementary teacher preparation.* Washington, DC: Author.

Available at www.ncate.org/standard/elemstds.pdf (last visited February 27, 2003).

National Council for Accreditation of Teacher Education. 2001. *Standards for professional development schools.* Washington, DC: Author.

National Council for Accreditation of Teacher Education. 2002. *Professional standards for the accreditation of schools, colleges, and departments of education* (2002 ed.). Washington, DC: Author.

National Council for the Social Studies. 2000. *Program standards for the initial preparation of social studies teachers.* Washington, DC: Author.

National Council of Teachers of Mathematics. 1998 (October). *NCATE program standards: Program for initial preparation of K–4 teachers with an emphasis in mathematics, 5–8 mathematics teachers, 7–12 mathematics teachers.* Reston, VA: Author. Available at www.ncate.org/standard/new%20program%20standards/nctm%202001.pdf (last visited February 27, 2003).

National Foundation for the Improvement of Education. Undated. *Changing teaching: The next frontier. A new vision of the profession.* Washington, DC: Author.

National Middle School Association. 1995. *This we believe: Developmentally responsive middle level schools.* Columbus, OH: Author.

National Middle School Association. 2001. *Middle level teacher preparation standards.* Westerville, OH: Author. Available at www.ncate.org/standard/new%20program%20standards/nmsa.pdf (last visited February 27, 2003).

National Science Teachers Association & Association for the Education of Teachers in Science. 1998 (November). *Standards for science teacher preparation.* Arlington, VA: Author. Available at www.nsta.org/main/pdfs/nsta98standards.pdf (last visited February 27, 2003).

Palmer, P. J. 1998. *The courage to teach.* San Francisco: Jossey-Bass.

Reiman, A. J., and L. Thies-Sprinthall. 1998. *Mentoring and supervision for teacher development.* New York: Addison-Wesley Longman.

Smart, R. C., Jr., et al. 1996. *Guidelines for the preparation of teachers of English language arts (1996 ed.).* Urbana, IL: National Council of Teachers of English.

Sprinthall, N. A., A. J. Reiman, and L. Thies-Sprinthall. 1996. "Teacher professional development." In J. Sikula, T. Buttery, and E. Guyton, eds., *Handbook of research on teacher education* (2nd ed.), 667–703. New York: Macmillan.

Teacher Education Accreditation Council. 2002. *TEAC accreditation process.* Available at www.teac.org/accreditation/index.asp (last visited February 27, 2003).

Tozer, S., T. H. Anderson, and B. B. Armbruster, eds. 1990. *Foundational studies in teacher education: A reexamination.* New York: Teachers College Press.

U.S. Department of Education. 2002. *Strategic plan 2002–2007.* Washington, DC: Author.

Wang, J., and S. J. Odell. 2002. "Mentoring learning to teach according to standards-based reform: A critical review." *Review of Educational Research*, 72, 481–546.

Wasley, P. A. 1991. *Teachers who lead: The rhetoric of reform and the realities of practice.* New York: Teachers College Press.

ABOUT
THE AUTHORS

Roy A. Edelfelt was the sole author of the first three editions of *Careers in Education*. Alan J. Reiman has coauthored this edition.

Dr. Reiman has had several careers in education. While studying for his undergraduate degree at Iowa State University from 1971 to 1975, he was actively involved in student personnel work, serving full-time as a residence hall adviser and part-time as the first student liaison to parents of incoming students.

From Iowa State, Mr. Reiman went to the University of Georgia, where he earned a master's degree. Subsequently he taught in rural elementary schools in Georgia and North Carolina for eight years. During that time he coedited a book on enrichment activities for elementary-school-age children. Also, he became interested in new teaching roles, such as mentor and curriculum designer. These interests eventually prompted him to earn a doctorate at North Carolina State University (NC State).

Dr. Reiman then took a position as clinical assistant professor, a joint appointment with NC State and the Wake County (North Carolina) Public Schools. In that position his primary focus was design, implementation, and evaluation of an innovative mentor support program for beginning teachers. Experiences from 1988 to 1995 provided him with an opportunity to blend teaching, administration, and program evaluation. During these years he was promoted to clinical associate professor.

In 1995, Dr. Reiman joined the faculty of NC State as an assistant professor. In this role he has coordinated master's and doctoral work in curriculum and instruction. In 2002 he was promoted to associate professor. Currently he also is coordinator of assessment for NC State's College of Education.

Dr. Reiman has authored more than seventy-five papers and two books. His articles have been published in many national and international journals.

Dr. Edelfelt also has had several careers in education. After graduating from the Crane School of Music at the State University of New York (SUNY) at Potsdam, and after a three-and-a-half-year stint in the U.S. Navy, he taught instrumental music in the public schools of Kingston, New York. While employed in Kingston, Dr. Edelfelt earned a master's degree at New York University. He then took a position at SUNY Oneonta as an instructor and a consultant in the college's laboratory school, a demonstration facility for K–9 teaching.

Through experiences at Oneonta with a program of integrated studies for the preparation of teachers, Dr. Edelfelt became convinced of the value of integrated studies in education, particularly in elementary schools. As a consequence, he enrolled in the doctoral program at Teachers College, Columbia University, specializing in curriculum and teaching.

On graduation, Dr. Edelfelt became an assistant professor at Saint Cloud State College (Minnesota). Later he was an associate professor at Michigan State University.

In 1962, Dr. Edelfelt left higher education to become associate executive secretary of the National Education Association's National Commission on Teacher Education and Professional Standards. This was the first of several leadership roles that he assumed in teacher education at the national level. Subsequently he became executive secretary of the commission. Later he served as a senior associate in the organization's Division of Instruction and Professional Development.

In the early 1980s, Dr. Edelfelt became a freelance consultant. He later became a clinical professor at The University of North Carolina at Chapel Hill (1989–2001) and an adjunct professor at NC State (1991–). He has authored, coauthored, or edited more than ten books and has published in many professional journals. Further, he has conducted and reported on numerous studies in the United States and overseas.